J. R. R. TOLKIEN
FOR KIDS

HIS LIFE AND WRITINGS, WITH 21 ACTIVITIES

SIMONETTA CARR

CHICAGO
REVIEW
PRESS

Copyright © 2021 Simonetta Carr
All rights reserved
First edition
Published by Chicago Review Press Incorporated
814 North Franklin Street
Chicago, Illinois 60610
ISBN 978-1-64160-346-1

Library of Congress Control Number: 2021938783

Cover design: Preston Pisellini
Cover images: FRONT: Battle of the Somme and
J. R. R. Tolkien with pipe, Alamy; Hobbiton,
Thomas Schweighofer / Unsplash; map of
Middle-earth, Alamy. BACK: Sarehole Mill and
Middle Earth Festival participant dressed as orc,
Paul Lucas / Flickr; runes, Pearson Scott Foresman /
Wikimedia Commons; Ents, Ted Nasmuth;
Tolkien with King Edward's School house group,
The King Edward's Foundation Archive.
Interior design: Sarah Olson
Interior illustrations: Jim Spence
Map design: Chris Erichsen

Printed in the United States of America
5 4 3 2 1

CONTENTS

TIME LINE

1892 January 3, John Ronald Reuel Tolkien born in Bloemfontein, South Africa

1894 February 17, Tolkien's younger brother, Hilary, is born

1895 Mabel Tolkien returns to England with her two boys

1896 February 15, Arthur Tolkien dies in Bloemfontein

Mabel Tolkien rents a cottage near Sarehole Mill, Moseley, near Birmingham

1900 Mabel accepted into the Roman Catholic Church

Ronald enrolls in King Edward's School

1904 Mabel diagnosed with diabetes and dies in November

Tolkien boys become wards of Father Morgan at the Birmingham Oratory

1905 Aunt Beatrice Suffield takes the boys into her home

1908 Tolkien boys move into a boarding house run by Mrs. Faulkner

Ronald meets Edith Bratt, another young lodger

1909 Father Francis Morgan discovers the romance between Ronald and Edith

1910 Tolkien brothers move to new lodgings

Edith Bratt moves to Cheltenham

1911 Start of the Tea Club and Barrovian Society

Tolkien begins his studies at Oxford

1913 Ronald writes to Edith on his 21st birthday, and they become engaged

1915 Tolkien applies for a temporary commission in the army and is posted to the 13th Battalion of the Lancashire Fusiliers, a reserve training unit

1916 March 22, Ronald and Edith married in Warwick

July 1, Tolkien, reassigned to the 11th Batallion, fights in World War I at the Battle of the Somme, France

November, Tolkien returns to England to recover from trench fever

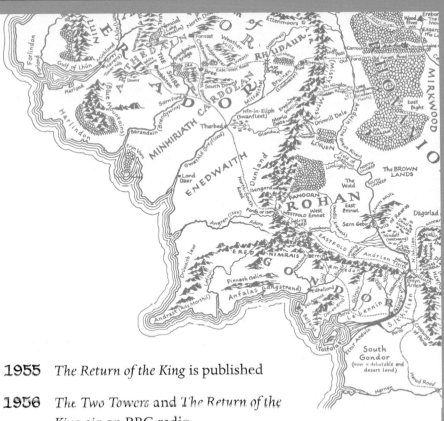

1917 Tolkien works on *The Book of Lost Tales*

November 16, the Tolkiens' eldest son, John, is born

1918 Tolkien joins staff of the *Oxford English Dictionary*

1920 Tolkien appointed Reader in English Language at Leeds University

October 22, the Tolkiens' second son, Michael, is born

1921 Edith, John, and Michael, join Tolkien at Leeds

1924 November 21, the Tolkiens' third son, Christopher, is born

1925 Tolkien elected professor of Anglo-Saxon at Oxford

1926 Tolkien's family joins him at Oxford

Tolkien befriends C. S. Lewis.

1929 June 18, Tolkien's daughter, Priscilla, is born

1930 Tolkien begins work on *The Hobbit*

1937 *The Hobbit* is published

Tolkien begins work on a sequel, *The Lord of the Rings*

1945 Tolkien becomes Merton Professor of English Language and Literature at Oxford

1949 Tolkien finishes writing *The Lord of the Rings*

1954 *The Fellowship of the Ring* and *The Two Towers* are published

1955 *The Return of the King* is published

1956 *The Two Towers* and *The Return of the King* air on BBC radio

1959 Tolkien retires from teaching

1968 The Tolkiens move to Poole, near Bournemouth

1971 Edith Tolkien dies

1972 March, Tolkien returns to Oxford and receives his CBE from the Queen

June, Oxford University awards Tolkien an honorary Doctorate of Letters

1973 September 2, Tolkien dies from a stomach ulcer

I

FROM AFRICAN DESERTS TO A LOST PARADISE

THE WORLD ON which John Ronald Reuel Tolkien first opened his eyes was thousands of miles away from the land of his ancestors. His parents, Arthur Reuel Tolkien and Mabel Suffield, were a young English couple living in Bloemfontein, South Africa. Arthur had moved there for work. Mabel had followed him for love.

Bloemfontein, around the year 1898.

Hilton Teper

Compared to Birmingham, their English hometown, Bloemfontein was a small village, surrounded by wide expanses of parched land where wolves, wild dogs, jackals, and lions roamed free. Mabel found it difficult to adjust.

FAIRY AND ELF

There was no room for grievances when their first child entered the world on the night of January 3, 1892—a summer night in the Southern Hemisphere. Arthur wrote immediately to his mother, describing the baby's beautiful features. As most parents do, he tried to find resemblances. His son had Tolkien eyes, he said, a Suffield mouth, and looked a lot like Arthur's sister.

Writing to her in-laws some time later, Mabel made a different association. When her son was all dressed up with the white ruffles and laces that were typical of baby clothes at the time—for both boys and girls—she said he looked like a fairy. Without them, he looked like an elf. Her words were almost prophetic, describing a boy who would one day open up a realm of fairies and elves to a generation hungry for better worlds.

The first name was an easy choice: John, the same as both Arthur's and Mabel's fathers. In the Tolkien family, it had been passed on from generation to generation. There was some discussion about a second name. Arthur wanted to pass on his middle name, Reuel, which meant "Friend of God." Mabel wanted the name Ronald, after the hero of Medieval tales. It would be the first time this name was used in their families. In the end, they kept both middle names, but Ronald would become their favorite of the two—so much so that they usually called their son Ronald instead of John.

DREAMS OF ENGLAND

Motherhood intensified Mabel's struggle with Africa's unique challenges. Snakes had to be kept out of the house, and a large spider bit Ronald soon after the boy started to walk. Once, a neighbor's pet monkey climbed over the wall and chewed up three of Ronald's outfits. Mabel also felt out of place in Bloemfontein's European community and was particularly upset at its racist treatment of the native population.

The Anglican Cathedral of St. Andrew and St. Michael, Bloemfontein, where J. R. R. Tolkien was baptized on January 31, 1892. *Grobler du Preez, iStock*

Her second son, Hilary Arthur Reuel, was born two years after Ronald and appeared to be quite healthy. Meanwhile, though, Ronald was suffering from frequent teething fevers. Mabel was concerned that the intense summer heat didn't agree with Ronald's constitution. Arthur, on the other hand, seemed quite comfortable in his new location—much to the concern of Mabel, who continued to hope for a transfer back to England.

When he was not working, Arthur liked to spend time with his children. Many years later, Ronald remembered watching him as he tended to the large garden behind their house, with its vines, cypresses, fir trees, and cedars. This may have been the start of Ronald's lifelong love for trees.

From time to time, Arthur took Ronald to the bank where he worked, allowing his son to sit at a desk to draw—a passion that continued throughout Ronald's life. As soon as he learned to talk, Ronald loved to entertain the clerks with his conversations. Since Bloemfontein was a small town, people had time to socialize.

As much as he enjoyed spending time with his children, though, Arthur understood Mabel's concerns about the effect the weather was having on both her health and Ronald's. He helped her plan a visit to her family in England, with the intention of joining her as soon as his business allowed it.

FIRST TRAVELS AND SORROWS

The departure date was set for the spring, but Mabel was not about to watch Ronald suffer

Bloemfontein

When Ronald was born, Bloemfontein was the capital of the Orange Free State, which became part of the nation of South Africa in 1910. Founded in 1846, Bloemfontein was built on a tableland about 4,500 feet (1,370 m) above sea level. It was considered a healthy location because it seldom rained, with just 70 days of showers in its most rainy year. But Mabel found the temperature range too extreme: it could go from 80.0°F (26°C) in January to 20.0°F (–7°C) in June.

The Tolkiens lived in a place known as Bank House, with the offices of the Bank of Africa, where Arthur worked, positioned under their living quarters. The building was located on Maitland Street, near the market square. The Parliament House, the hospital, and the **Anglican** Cathedral that the Tolkiens attended were in the same general area.

through another sweltering summer. In November, just before the hottest months, she took the boys to the coast near Cape Town, where the climate was milder. Later in life, Ronald remembered sitting during the long train ride, running on the flat sandy shore, and bathing in the ocean.

They returned to Bloemfontein in time to make their last preparations for the trip. They boarded SS *Guelph* on March 29, 1895. Many years later, Ronald still pictured the ship leaving the dock, with passengers throwing out coins for good luck and a group of local children diving in the water to find them.

A view of Cape Town from a nearby island. The coast near Cape Town is famous for its high waves. *Portland Seminary, Flickr*

Wide open spaces near Bloemfontein, something Tolkien loved and missed. *Stephen Downes, Flickr*

As the ship moved away, the land where Ronald was born gradually became a distant blur—a place he remembered with fondness, even if much of it was hot and barren. Almost fifty years later, he told his son that, as much as he loved the green meadows and trees of England, wide spaces—such as the seemingly endless stretches of African land—continued to fill him with awe. Many years later, when he wrote the first dictionary for the Elvish languages he created, he called Africa Salkinor ("Grass Land") and Andisalkë ("Long Grass").

One image from the last moments before his departure remained especially imprinted in Ronald's mind: his father painting the words A. R. TOL-KIEN on a family trunk. This was his last memory of Arthur, who became seriously ill in November, from either typhoid or rheumatic fever.

By the start of the new year, Arthur's illness was serious enough to prompt Mabel to buy tickets back to Africa. Ronald, barely four years old, dictated a letter addressed to his father, telling him how much he was looking forward to seeing him. But Arthur died the day after his son's letter was written, before anyone could mail it. He was buried in the President Brand Cemetery in Bloemfontein.

A BRAVE NEW WORLD

Mabel Tolkien's life changed overnight. At 26 years old, she suddenly found herself a single mother, dealing with a heavy burden of grief while looking for new accommodations and planning her children's education. The accommodations came first.

They had been staying with Mabel's parents in a neighborhood just outside Birmingham, called King's Heath. Being so young, sometimes Ronald mixed images in his mind. For the rest of his life, he remembered a house that didn't actually exist, because it was a combination of his house in Bloemfontein and his grandparents' home in Birmingham.

Ronald and Hilary enjoyed the warm hospitality of Grandmother Emily and the funny antics of Grandfather John, an energetic man with a bushy beard. But the place was overcrowded, as two of Mabel's siblings and a lodger shared the same home.

Mabel's funds were limited to a few small shares from investments Arthur had made in South African mines. In spite of this, in the summer of 1896 she was able to find an affordable house for rent in the rural community of Sarehole, about two miles east of King's Heath, where the boys could benefit from the fresh air and contact with nature.

Like most children at that time, Ronald and Hilary were free to explore their surroundings—a world radically different from anything they had experienced in either Bloemfontein or Birmingham, and a world they would never forget.

They spent hours following small paths, running through fields and walking uphill to a favorite sandpit and a small, wooded area they named Bumble Dell, from the local word for blackberry, a fruit that grew wild there. Bumble Dell was a delightful place, full of berries, mushrooms,

How Small Can You Write?

Mabel's father, John, liked to entertain the children with fun jokes and small challenges. Sometimes, he would draw a circle around a sixpence coin (about the same size of a US penny) and write the entire text of the Lord's Prayer (about 65 words) inside the circle. How many words can you fit inside the same circle?

YOU'LL NEED

* Paper
* Penny
* Mechanic pencil or very sharp pencil
* Eraser

1. Place a sheet of paper on a clean surface, then place a penny in the middle of it. Hold it down with a finger of the hand you don't use to write.

2. With your other hand, use the pencil to draw a circle around the penny.

3. Remove the penny and try to write the Lord's Prayer, or anything else you like that's about 65 words, inside the circle. Write as small as you can. Use an eraser to correct mistakes. Tip: if you write the words in a spiral, you will probably be able to fit more.

4. Count how many words you were able to fit inside the circle.

5. (Optional) Challenge your friends to try this activity and compare results.

orchids, and rabbits. It was probably Moseley Bog, a drained artificial lake where vegetation was allowed to grow wild. Soon, Ronald knew the area so well that he could have drawn a map.

Ronald and Hilary were especially fascinated by a nearby brick building known as Sarehole Mill. They liked to stare at the waterfall that caused the milling wheel to turn and at the wild swans swimming in the pond. Sometimes they moved to the yard to watch the sacks of flour fall onto an open cart below or ventured to peek through an opening into the dark rooms inside, with all the noisy machinery and busy activity.

If the two millers, a father and son, spotted the boys, the younger miller would regularly chase

The pond behind Sarehole Mill. *Paul Lucas, Flickr*

them away. Since this miller wore white dusty clothes, Ronald nicknamed him "White Ogre." This ogre seemed to be constantly annoyed with the boys—whether they spied inside the mill or walked through his fields of wheat and barley.

But he was not the only person to send them running. Not far from the mill, there was a farmer the boys called "Black Ogre," who chased them if he caught them picking mushrooms on his land. The boys thought that, of the two ogres, the black one was the meaner. He would confiscate the shoes and socks of any child he caught paddling on the stream by his house. If they asked to have them back, he would give them a good beating. But going home without shoes could produce the same results, so the boys had a difficult decision to make. Years later, Hilary said he wondered what the Black Ogre did with all those shoes.

Sometimes the boys deserved some scolding—for example, the times they teased a Mr. Heaven, who had a daughter named Hellen, by asking, "How is Hell-in Heaven?" Mr. Heaven would then chase them around the lake with a sharp pointed stick, until they reached the place where the swans were nesting. At that point, he could leave the punishment to the swans, which would nip at the boys' pants. One time, however, a swan decided to protect the boys and turned against Mr. Heaven instead.

Making friends with other children was not always easy. Ronald and Hilary spoke with a more refined accent than the locals. That, together with their long hair and their fancy clothes, made them seem ridiculous to the country boys.

Turn a Blade of Grass into a Whistle

In Sarehole, the Tolkien boys used to make whistles out of reeds. Since reeds are not found everywhere and carving them requires a sharp knife, this activity will teach you another way to make a whistle.

YOU'LL NEED

❋ Blade of grass

1. Pick a blade of grass that is straight and even. It should be at least as long as your thumb.

2. Place the blade against one of your thumbs. Hold it in place at the top with your index finger and at the bottom with your ring finger.

2. Place your other thumb against the first as shown and move the ring finger away. You may also move your index finger, as long as your thumbs are holding the blade of grass firmly.

3. Put your mouth on the hole between your hands where the blade of grass appears and blow. If at first you don't succeed, try again. You might need to reposition the blade or move your hands slightly.

You can experiment by using a blade of grass that is thicker or thinner. Or you may try opening your other fingers, cupping them closer together, or opening and closing them while you blow to produce different sounds.

The River Cole near Tolkien's home floods easily during heavy rains. Some believe that memories of these flash floods might have lingered in Tolkien's mind when he described the flood that washed away the Black Riders in *The Lord of the Rings*. *bobistraveling, Flickr*

A coin celebrating Queen Victoria's Diamond Jubilee. The inscription reads, "Victoria happily closes the 60th year of her reign, 20 June 1897." Ronald remembered how the school near his Sarehole home was decorated for the occasion with hundreds of colorful lights. *Copyright Chards.co.uk, published with permission*

At the same time, Ronald and Hilary disliked the boys' rough manners.

Eventually, the Tolkien boys did pick up some of the local words, such as "miskin" for trash can and "gamgee" for cotton wool (from the name of its inventor, Sampson Gamgee). This last word inspired the last name of one of the heroes Ronald would describe years later in his famous work, *The Lord of the Rings*.

LANGUAGES, DRAGONS, AND TREES

Mabel provided her sons more than a beautiful place to live. From a young age, she taught them to appreciate literature, to study the meaning and origin of words, to draw and paint, to explore different types of handwriting, to use proper grammar, and to learn different languages. She taught them how to step into worlds of imagination, showing them that there is more to life than what human eyes can see, and gave them tools to describe what they imagined. By example, she communicated her passion for learning and creating.

Ronald appreciated some school subjects more than others. He liked learning Latin and German but was not particularly interested in studying French or playing the piano. He enjoyed history and science but was less drawn to math, which was not one of Mabel's strong subjects either.

By age four, Ronald had already learned how to read. With time, he came to appreciate many of the popular children's books of his day, such as Lewis Carroll's *Alice's Adventures in Wonderland*,

Create an Elegant Handwriting Style

*Mabel's handwriting was unusual and refined, with capital letters enriched by elaborate curls and vertical lines that changed direction, moving horizontally over the word. Ronald learned from her but developed his own style—different but equally elegant. Throughout his life, he remained interested in different types of handwriting, including Medieval **calligraphy** and floral alphabets.*

In this activity, you will create your own handwriting style.

YOU'LL NEED

❋ Internet access or a book on handwriting

❋ Sheet of penmanship paper (from a book or from an online template)

❋ Pencil

❋ Eraser

❋ Pen (optional)

1. With an adult's permission, use the Internet or a book on handwriting to find a sample of cursive writing that you like. Following this sample, try to write a short letter in a similar cursive style.

2. Try to make the letters more elaborate by adding curls and swirling lines.

3. (Optional) When you are satisfied with your handwriting, trace over it with a pen. Make sure the pen does not smudge. After the ink dries, erase the pencil marks underneath.

BONUS: To experience the way Ronald wrote, purchase a dip pen and ink online or at an art supply store. This will allow you to make your lines thinner or thicker by pressing less or more on the nib. (Make sure you keep the ink away from books, carpets, and other objects that might become damaged by spills. Also keep some paper towels nearby.)

George MacDonald's *The Princess and the Goblin*, and Andrew Lang's Fairy Books. He relished the tales of King Arthur and wished he could visit his court. One of his favorite stories was about a hero named Sigurd who slew the dragon Fáfnir. He discovered later that it was taken from an Icelandic saga named *Völsunga*, a story he continued to explore for much of his life.

He eventually decided to write a story of his own, about a green great dragon. Mabel corrected him. She explained that we say "a *great green* dragon," not the other way around. Ronald never discovered the reason behind this rule, but he became curious to find similar ones. Later, he would say his mother was the first one to inspire his love for languages.

Tolkien's love for science went along with his desire to explore nature around him. He enjoyed books about plants, animals, and stars and continued to feel a deep fondness for trees. He liked climbing trees, learning their names, talking to them, and drawing them, and he was a very good artist.

One of the greatest disappointments of his life in Sarehole was when someone cut down one of his favorite climbing trees—an old willow hanging over the mill pool. What's worse, he realized that no one used the tree. They just left it there to die, destroyed for no apparent reason. He never forgot this painful discovery. Sadly, many more were to follow, especially after he moved to the city.

The Order of Adjectives

As Ronald discovered, in English a list of adjectives follows a specific order—probably because that's the way people have normally organized them. Barring a few exceptions, the basic order is as follows:

1. Possessive (your, his, her, my, their, our) and demonstrative adjectives (this, that, those, these), articles and numbers or quantifiers (ten, some, many).
2. Observation or opinion (beautiful, exciting, strange)
3. Size (small, large, huge)
4. Shape (square, triangular, round)
5. Age (old, young, ancient)
6. Color (yellow, red, green)
7. Origin or nationality (American, British, Californian)
8. Material (wooden, plastic, steel)
9. Qualifier—a noun that is used as an adjective to indicate the type of noun (evening gown, cell phone, hand shadows) or an adjective ending with "ing" that describes the purpose of the noun (vending machine, hiking shoes, walking stick).

Now you can pay more attention to lists of adjectives you read. Are most writers following these rules?

Make a Shadowy Dragon Come to Life

While Tolkien never talked about hand shadows, this was a favorite pastime of children of his day, before the invention of cell phones and computer games. All you need to make hand shadows is a source of light, a clear wall, two hands, and a lot of imagination.

YOU'LL NEED

❈ Two hands

❈ Desk lamp (or other source of light)

❈ Clear wall

1. Make your left hand into the shape of a C.

2. Slide your middle finger back to create a triangle over the other fingers. This will be the eye of your dragon.

3. Lower your little finger so that it is positioned between the thumb and the other fingers. This will be your dragon's tongue, as shown.

4. Position your hand between the wall and the source of light, until you see a shadow on the wall. It should look like the head of a snake.

5. Join your right arm to the left and grab your left hand so that your right thumb is against the palm of the left hand. Position the other fingers of your right hand to make them look like scales on the back of the dragon's head.

6. Wiggle the left-hand little finger to make your dragon move its tongue.

You may have to move your hand in different directions until you find the perfect shadow on the wall. You might want to try out entirely new ideas. Be creative!

If hand-shadow art interests you, you can look at your local library for books about it or look online for tutorials.

2

CHANGES AND HEARTBREAKS

T HE YEAR 1900 marked a series of important changes in Ronald's life, starting with his mother's faith. After their wedding, Mabel and Arthur had attended services at an Anglican Church, and Mabel continued to do the same in her own country. Just before the turn of the century, however, her views began to change.

In the King Edward's Cadet Corps, Ronald learned basic military drills. Even though England was not at war, this type of training was encouraged for all young men in good learning institutions (who had potential to become officers). This picture was taken on April 4, 1907. Ronald is in the second row from the bottom, the second young man to the right of the principal. *The King Edward's Foundation Archive*

She discussed her thoughts with her sister May Incledon, who had also been living in South Africa and had just returned to England for a visit. Together, they began to receive instruction in the Roman Catholic religion at St. Anne's Church in the busy center of Birmingham. Soon, they decided to join that church.

For many people today, it's hard to understand what this decision meant in England at the turn of the 20th century. Ever since the 16th century, when King Henry VIII broke away from the Roman Catholic Church and placed himself at the head of the Church of England (or Anglican Church), the struggle between Protestants and

The Oxford Movement

The founder of St. Anne's Church was John Henry Newman, a former Anglican who had converted to Roman Catholicism. He was one of the leaders of a group known as the "Oxford Movement," which emphasized the Catholic roots of the Church of England. Newman, along with the other leaders of the movement, believed the Church of England had become too individualistic, making personal experience more important than church institutions, tradition, and **sacraments**.

When Newman went so far as to say that the 39 Articles of Religion—a foundational document of the Church of England written during the Protestant Reformation—was not in contradiction with Roman Catholicism, the Oxford Movement met the Church of England's final disapproval.

Newman went on to become a cardinal in the Roman Catholic Church. On October 13, 2019, he was canonized as a Roman Catholic saint.

Cardinal John Henry Newman in 1874. *From Wilfrid Ward, The Life of John Henry Cardinal Newman (London: Longsman, Greens & Co., 1912). Engraving by Joseph Brown. Scanned by Julian Felsenburgh, Wikimedia Commons.*

St. Anne's Church. *Tony Hisgett, Wikimedia Commons*

Roman Catholics in England had been so constant that becoming Catholic was almost considered an act of disloyalty to the country.

Both sides of Ronald's family, the Tolkiens and the Suffields, were shocked by Mabel's decision. They were probably sincerely concerned for Mabel and her sons but, instead of simply reasoning this out with Mabel, most of them chose to disown her.

May's husband, who was still in South Africa, was deeply upset by May's choice and forbade her to enter a Roman Catholic church ever again. In those days, husbands were thought to have the authority to make such demands, and May complied. (She later turned to spiritualism, the practice of communicating with the dead.) Mabel, being a widow, stood her ground, but she lost both the acceptance and the financial support of her family.

LIFE IN THE CITY

Only one uncle continued to support Mabel and her boys. In September, with the uncle's financial help, Mabel enrolled eight-year-old Ronald at King Edward's School, the best school in Birmingham—the same school that her husband, Arthur, had attended as a child.

Initially, Ronald walked four miles to and from school every day, because Mabel could not afford to pay for the train. Walking such a distance was not unusual for children at that time.

Eventually, Mabel decided to move closer to the center of Birmingham, where her small family could easily walk to church and school. Though

Means of Transportation

At the end of the 19th century, many people in England still rode horses or used stagecoaches to move from place to place and used animal-drawn carts to move goods. A popular means of transportation within cities were horse-drawn **trams** (or horsecars), which ran on special steel rails known as "tramways." There were other options, however.

The rail system was developed in the 1820s and progressed rapidly until, by the time Ronald lived in Sarehole, it boasted efficient railways all over the country.

Modern cars were first developed in the 1860s but were not ready for sale until the end of the century. In 1903, the American Henry Ford introduced the Model T Ford, which began to be mass produced five years later.

Birmingham was an industrial city, the parts of town where they lived were not far from the country and were rich in parks, gardens, and trees.

Still, Ronald never forgot Sarehole's magic and beauty. To him, Sarehole remained a place like no other. Many years later, he said that the Shire, the place the Hobbits in his books called home, was largely inspired by his childhood memories—especially those he lived at Sarehole.

The Tolkiens couldn't rent their first house for long, because it was demolished to make room for a fire station. Their second home was next to King's Heath Station, a busy place where the family had to put up with the smoke of coal engines and the noise of trains and trucks, and the people who boarded them, loaded, and unloaded them. Ronald was especially fascinated by the strange names on the coal trucks—names like Nantygio, Senghenydd, Blaen-Rhondda, Perhiweeiber, and Tredegar. He discovered these were names of towns in Wales. Out of curiosity, he looked for books written in Welsh and found the language both intriguing and incomprehensible.

Mabel's search for a good Roman Catholic church near her new location led her to Birmingham Oratory, founded by Cardinal John Henry

Newman, who had lived and died there. Some of the priests in the oratory had served under Newman and shared much of his vision for the church. One of these was Father Francis Xavier Morgan, who became particularly important in Ronald's life.

Next to the oratory was the Grammar School of St. Philip, which was more affordable than King Edward's School and included Roman Catholic instruction. Mabel thought it was a good choice for her boys, so she transferred them there. She also found a home closer to the oratory and quieter than the place by the station.

Soon, it became obvious that St. Philip's courses were not challenging enough for Ronald, who had already received an extensive education. He was able to move back to King Edward's without much of a wait, while Hilary had to wait a couple of years before he could pass the better school's entrance test.

A SPECIAL LOVE FOR LANGUAGES

The teachers at King Edward's nurtured Ronald's passion for languages. Besides the customary Latin and Greek, which were part of every high school curriculum, they gave him a taste of Middle English (used in England between the 12th and 15th centuries) and Old English (spoken at the time of the Norman conquest of 1066).

In the meantime, Ronald continued to learn as much as he could about other ancient languages of northern Europe, such as Welsh, Finnish, Norse, and Gothic, and about the connections between

King's Heath Station. *Geoff Dowling, used with permission*

them. Of all these, Gothic was his first true passion, so much so that he decorated his books with Gothic script and marked them with a Gothicized version of his name: Ruginwaldus Dwalakôncis.

Some of these languages attracted him because of their sounds. In other cases, he wanted to read the original versions of some of the stories he had come to love, including the *Kalevala*, a 19th-century Finnish epic poem. He wanted to hear the heroes of those exciting ancient stories as they would sound in real life.

As if all the existing languages were not enough, Ronald tried to invent new ones. Mabel disapproved of this pastime, as it distracted him from his school assignments. But for Ronald, this was more than simply a fun activity or a way to communicate secretly with friends. It was a creative way of putting into practice what he was learning from books and using a talent that he could not repress.

For many, Ronald's love for languages may be difficult to understand. It was more than a simple interest or curiosity. It was a passion that sprung from an unusual skill, like a musician's ability to recognize sounds and develop them in new, original ways, or a painter's ability to see and create images.

But it was even more unique. While most writers and philologists can understand and enjoy words and their sounds, and many can combine them in pleasant and creative ways, few are as skilled as Ronald would become at recognizing sounds and understanding the way languages work. Even fewer people can develop ancient,

King Edward's School in 1894.
Wikimedia Commons (from Robert Kirkup Dent, The Making of Birmingham: Being a History of the Rise and Growth of the Midland Metropolis, Birmingham, J. L. Allday).

forgotten languages, or take existing languages and create new ones, while keeping logical links to the others and flawless structure.

For example, when Ronald couldn't find enough written records to allow him to express himself in Gothic, he created new words that were consistent with the existing ones, following the same structures he had observed in the words and grammar he already knew. To accomplish this, he had to really study the records of Gothic and even try to imagine how the language might have sounded in earlier stages of its development. Most people would find this task exhausting. He found it thrilling.

WHAT IS HOME WITHOUT A MOTHER?

The winter of 1904 was particularly difficult for the Tolkien family. First, the boys came down with measles and then with whooping cough. To make things worse, Hilary developed pneumonia. Mabel, also feeling ill and weary, struggled to care for them. Eventually, the boys recovered, but Mabel's health continued to deteriorate.

By April, Mabel had to be admitted to a hospital, where she was diagnosed with diabetes. Insulin, today's common remedy against this illness, had not yet been discovered, so she could only rest and watch her diet.

For a while, Hilary stayed with his grandparents while Ronald stayed with Edwin Neave, the future husband of his aunt Jane. Ronald sent frequent drawings and notes to his mother to encourage and amuse her. One of these showed a hint of sadness. Titled "What is Home Without a Mother (or a Wife)," it depicted Ronald and Edwin sitting by a fire, one mending a pair of pants and the other knitting a sock. By portraying an unmarried man and a boy separated from his mother performing some traditionally feminine tasks, Ronald communicated their loneliness and need.

When Mabel left the hospital in late June, Father Francis found two small rooms in a restful place where she and the boys could live together: Woodside Cottage, near the village of Rednal, where Cardinal Newman had built a retreat for the priests at the oratory. Father Francis arranged

(above) **Mr. A. E. Measure's house group. Tolkien is third from the left in the front row. House groups were meant to provide the students with support and personal supervision.** *The King Edward's Foundation Archive*

(right) **Lickey Hills Park, near Rednal, less than ten miles southwest of Birmingham, was one of the delightful places the Tolkien boys could explore while their mother was recovering. The whole area is still rural and rich in trees.** *Roger Cutler, Flickr*

for the owners of the cottage to provide the Tolkien family with everything they needed, he and visited as often as he could.

Rednal was a lovely place to spend the summer. It gave the boys plenty of woods to explore, trees to climb, berries to pick, and open fields for running and flying kites—temporary distractions from the painful reality of their mother's suffering.

When schools reopened in September, Mabel decided to stay at Woodside Cottage for the sake of her health. This meant that 12-year-old Ronald had to get up early, walk more than a mile to Rednal, take a train to Birmingham, and walk again to

Some of Tolkien's Made-Up Languages

During a visit to Mabel's sister May, Ronald discovered that his cousins Marjorie and Mary had created a language they called Animalic—where they substituted names of animals for current words. He enthusiastically tried to learn it, even though he was not as fluent as they were.

This language was of course very limited, and eventually Marjorie lost interest. Ronald and Mary, instead, invented a new and more sophisticated one: Nevbosh, from the English "bosh," meaning "nonsense." It was based on languages they had learned, such as Latin and French, but also included new and unexpected sounds.

Later, Ronald took the project even further, moving from Nevbosh to Naffarin, a language with strong influences from Latin and Spanish, which he might have learned from Father Francis. Traces of this language have been found in Quenya, the Elvish language Ronald started to develop in 1915 and would later use in *The Lord of the Rings*.

While he was working on Quenya, Ronald developed a second Elvish language, which he eventually called Sindarin. In his later writings, Quenya, mostly inspired by Germanic and Finnish languages, became the Elvish language used for ceremonies, while Sindarin, inspired by Welsh, became the most commonly used tongue.

Ronald kept developing other languages for what he later called his "secondary world" and its inhabitants. Over time, this secondary world began to take shape in his mind. Once, later in his life, when someone asked him what *The Lord of the Rings* was all about, he told him "it was an effort to create a situation in which a common greeting would be *Elen síla lúmenn omentielvo*" ("A star shines on the hour of our meeting").

He noticed that, in some ancient legends, the names of the characters seemed to perfectly match the story, and he wanted to find the same perfect match, in his own tales, for the languages and names he created. In fact, often a name would bring up a story.

Build a Kite

The Tolkien boys enjoyed flying their kites in the wide fields outside of Birmingham. In those days, many children made their own kites. You can make one too.

YOU'LL NEED

- 2 bamboo dowels, measuring about ¼ inch (4 mm) in diameter and 24 inches in length
- Measuring tape
- Marker
- Strong scissors
- Twist tie (optional)
- 13-gallon white trash bag
- Scotch tape
- Ribbons (or long strips of tissue paper)
- Colored markers (optional)
- Nylon kite string (with handle attached), or thick sewing thread and an empty toilet paper roll

1. Measure one of the bamboo dowels and use your marker to mark the 20-inch (50-cm) mark.

2. Cut the dowel on that mark.

3. With the measuring tape, find the middle point of the shorter, 20-inch dowel and mark it.

4. Measure about 6 inches (15 cm) from the top of the longer, 24-inch dowel and mark this point.

5. Place the shorter dowel on top of the other so that the two marked points intersect, forming a cross.

6. Wrap and tie some string around the point where the straws intersect. You may use a twist-tie to make it stronger.

7. Press the sharp edge of a pair of scissors against each of the four dowel ends, making a notch in each that runs parallel with the surface the cross is resting on.

8. Wrap kite string around the cross at the dowel tips, making sure it rests inside the notches you have just created. Once you are done, cut the string and secure it with a knot, making sure the string is pulled taut around the tips of the cross.

9. Cut two sides of a trash bag so that it opens up entirely, then lay it on a clean surface.

10. Place your newly built frame on top of the trash bag, making sure the frame rests in the center.

11. Use a marker to draw a line onto the trash bag around the frame, at about a 1-inch (2.5 cm) distance from the frame. Remove the frame, then use scissors to cut out the resulting diamond shape.

12. (Optional) Decorate one side of the trash bag with your colored markers.

13. Flip the trash bag so that the decorations are on the underside, then place the frame back on top, in the center.

14. Fold the extra plastic over the frame, following the shape of the kite. Use tape to secure it.

15. Tie colored ribbons around the side ends and the bottom end of the dowels. Once you fly your kite, these ribbons will hang down from the kite's underside, adding color and style to your creation.

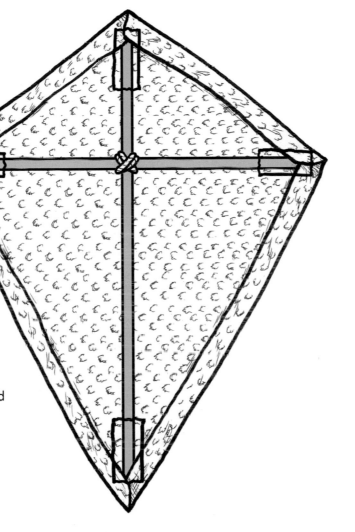

16. Tie the loose end of the nylon kite string to the center of your cross. Pull to make sure it's tied firmly. If you are not using string made for kites (that comes with a handle attached to one end), tie one end of your string to the center of the cross, then tie the other end around an empty roll of toilet paper. Pull both knots to make sure they're tied firmly, then wrap most of the string around the toilet paper roll. This will make it easy for you to unwrap it while you run.

17. Take your kite outside in an open field, preferably on a windy day. You may want to ask a friend to hold the kite while you start running and release it after you have caught some speed.

Create a Rebus

A rebus is a puzzle in which words are represented by a combination of images, letters, and numbers. This type of puzzle fascinates people who love to play with words, like Ronald did. On August 8, 1904, Ronald wrote a letter to Father Francis, using a combination of letters, numbers, and pictures instead of writing out each word. You can see the first page of the letter here: https://www.futilitycloset.com/2015/06/13/riddles-in-the-dark/. See if you can decipher any of it. If you can't, look at the answer below the image (on the same webpage).

Now, try solving another rebus.

YOU'LL NEED

❋ Paper

❋ Pencil or pen

1. Try to solve this rebus. The solution is below.

2. Now create a rebus of your own.

3. Send your rebus to some friends and see if they can figure out your message.

Solution: Can you see I love ice cream?

the school. By the time he came home in the evening, it was dark. Sometimes Hilary, who had still not gained admission into the school, met Ronald with a lamp to walk part of the way home with him. The boys gladly put up with the inconvenience because it was all for their mother's health.

Despite the boys' best efforts, though, Mabel's condition continued to worsen. In the beginning of November 1904, Mabel collapsed into a diabetic

Mabel Suffield Tolkien's grave, in the churchyard of St. Peter's Church at Bromsgrove, where the oratory priests were buried. Father Francis ordered that her tombstone follow the same design as that used for the priests'.
GentryGraves, Wikimedia Commons

coma. She died on November 14, 1904, at Woodside Cottage, with Father Francis and her sister May by her side. She was only 34.

Later in life, Ronald would reflect on his mother's death, resenting that so many of his relatives had abandoned her in this time of need. If she had received sufficient financial help, he thought, she might have been able to find better medical care. In fact, she could have taken better care of her health from the start if she had been able to afford some help with her family and chores. Years later, Ronald would remember Father Francis as the person who first taught him true charity and forgiveness—two virtues that he dearly needed in the wake of his mother's death.

ORPHANS

In her will, Mabel had appointed Father Francis as her sons' legal guardian. Religion was too important to her to leave them with members of her family, who would try to bring the boys back to a Protestant church. And religion was important to Ronald too. He understood the sacrifices his mother had made to pursue her faith, now more than ever before, and he was determined to follow on the path she had fought so hard to lay down for him and his brother.

But the Tolkien boys could not live in the oratory. For a while, they moved from relative to relative, spending a short time at the home of one of Arthur's brothers and then in the care of Aunt Beatrice Suffield, the widow of Mabel's brother William. Lacking strong religious convictions, Aunt Beatrice did not oppose the boys' commitment to Roman Catholicism.

Beatrice did not live far from the oratory, and the large upper room she gave the boys had a view of the countryside Ronald loved dearly. She was fairly indifferent to their feelings, though, so the boys felt more at home among the priests and other residents of the oratory.

A typical day for Ronald and Hilary began with their duties as altar boys during the daily Mass given by Father Francis, followed by breakfast at the cafeteria and then a bicycle ride to school, where they spent most of their daytime hours.

For a few summers, Father Francis took them on vacation to the sea resort of Lyme Regis, about 150 miles (240 km) south of Birmingham. Ronald loved exploring the area and drawing its sceneries on his sketchbook. One of the highlights of the vacations was his discovery of a petrified jawbone, which he imagined came from a dragon.

During one of these vacations, the boys confessed to Father Francis they were not happy staying with Aunt Beatrice, so the priest began to look for different accommodations. A few months later, he moved them to the home of a couple of parishioners, Mr. and Mrs. Faulkner, who lived on Duchess Road, close to the oratory. The Faulkners were already hosting another orphan, a bright young girl with a slender figure and dark hair and eyes, named Edith Bratt.

The boys found that Edith was easy to talk to, and she enjoyed their company too. She was fun and lively and loved to sing, dance, and play the piano. In fact, she dreamed of becoming a pianist.

A portion of the curving stone pier in Lyme Regis, known as the Cobb. *Tim Banting, Flickr*

The three developed a strong bond as orphans in a stranger's home and looked after one another. For example, when Edith learned that Mrs. Faulkner's meals were too small to satisfy the boys' hunger, she convinced the maid to bring her extra food. She then smuggled it to their room through a basket she lowered from her window to theirs, which was immediately below her own. Often, when Mrs. Faulkner was out, the boys would go to Edith's room and feast on whatever food she had hidden for them.

LOVE KINDLED

Edith and Ronald became particularly fond of each other. The fact that she was three years older than him did not seem to matter to either of them, because Ronald had grown in many ways past his age.

They began to spend more time together, riding bicycles, exploring their surroundings, and especially talking. They could talk for hours and never run out of things to say. Often, they talked from window to window—sometimes early in the morning, as the sun rose over town and the town's clock tolled out each hour. In fact, they developed a secret whistle call they could use when they wanted to talk to each other.

They also shared in small acts of mischief, such as sitting at a table on the top floor of a tea shop and throwing sugar cubes onto the hats of the unfortunate ladies who happened to be sitting under them. When their sugar bowl was empty, Edith and Ronald moved to another table and tormented another group.

After a year, they knew they were in love. Their first, almost accidental kiss sealed their relationship, although they tried to keep it secret.

All these new feelings and activities were bound to take their toll on Ronald's scholastic performance, and they did so at the worst possible time: he was supposed to be studying even harder to gain a scholarship to Oxford University, one of the best colleges in England.

To be fair, this was not the only distraction. He was a member of the cadet corps, the debating society, and the rugby team. Because of his shy personality and thin body, neither debating nor playing rugby came naturally to him, and he had to compensate for this lack of natural ability with many hours of practice.

On top of that, Ronald was still making up languages and discovering some that had become obsolete. In fact, in a letter he wrote years later, he confessed that creating languages was probably the greatest disturbance to his studies.

In any case, it was his relationship with Edith that caught the attention of Father Francis. Despite

What If?

In his debating society, Ronald once argued that England would have been better if, in 1066, the local Anglo-Saxons had defeated the Normans who invaded from France and imposed their lifestyle and language. This "what if" fantasy went along with Ronald's interest in Anglo-Saxon (or Old English) literature.

Try to do something similar.

YOU'LL NEED

❋ Paper

❋ Pencil or pen (or computer and printer)

1. Choose a historical event and imagine how history might have developed if this event had turned out differently. For example, what if the American colonies had failed in their revolution against England? Or what if Martin Luther King Jr. had survived the shooting that took his life?

2. Write down your thoughts.

3. Discuss them with your family, classmates, or friends. Explain why you think things would have been different in the way you described and listen to any objections or counterpoints. Did the discussion help everyone to see this event from different points of view?

their precautions of leaving and returning home separately, the young lovers were spotted together by a neighbor, who told the oratory's caretaker, who told the cook, who told Father Francis. After some investigation, the priest learned that Ronald and Edith had been getting closer for a while.

Father Francis believed he had to put a stop to this relationship. He was convinced that Ronald, as bright as he was, belonged in Oxford. But Ronald did not have the same financial advantages other students enjoyed, so if he was to attend the prestigious school, he would have to earn a scholarship. Father Francis knew Ronald could do it if he applied himself entirely to his studies.

With this conviction in mind, the priest moved Ronald and Hilary to new lodgings and demanded that Ronald put an end to his relationship with

The Lauterbrunnen Valley in Switzerland might have been the inspiration for Rivendell, a refuge hidden amid the mountains that Tolkien described in *The Lord of the Rings*. *Chensi-yuan, Wikimedia Commons*

Edith. Still in love, Ronald continued to meet Edith secretly. When Father Francis found out, he arranged for Edith to move to Cheltenham, about 50 miles (80 km) south of Birmingham, to live with friends of her family, known to her as Uncle and Aunt Jessop. The priest asked Ronald to cease all contact with Edith, even by letter, until he turned 21. Ronald's university career was at stake.

Initially, the separation yielded opposite results from what the Father had wanted. Instead of applying himself to his studies, Ronald became lethargic and distracted. With time, however, he understood that his future depended on his scholastic efforts. This realization, together with the debt of gratitude he felt toward Father Francis, helped him to apply himself to his studies.

Ronald's efforts were rewarded in December 1910, when he received the hoped-for scholarship to Oxford. It did not cover all of his expenses, but he was able to pay for some things with a little money Mabel had saved for his education. Father Francis covered the rest of Ronald's expenses with some of his family's earnings from a winery in Spain.

Hilary left King Edward's in June of the same year and went to work as clerk for one of his uncles. He and Ronald continued to live together until Ronald moved to Oxford.

A MEMORABLE TRIP

Ronald graduated from high school in the summer of 1911. Before starting college, he joined his brother Hilary, other relatives, and some family

friends in an unforgettable walking trip through the mountains of Switzerland. The unexpected beauty of the scenery left him awestruck. He had never seen anything like it.

The journey was full of adventures, including a night in a barn and a dangerous avalanche, when large stones and boulders came rolling down a slope, heading toward the travelers. One of these rocks missed Ronald by about a foot.

Many years later, some of these images would come back to his mind and become an inspiration for some of his writings. For example, the hobbits' journey he wrote about in *The Lord of the Rings*, from the Elven town of Rivendell to the other side of the Misty Mountains, was probably based on this trip through the Swiss Alps.

3

UNDERGRADUATE

WITH THE MEMORIES of this trip still vivid in his mind, Tolkien returned home, packed his belongings, and moved to the university. He arrived in early October in grand style, sitting in a "motor-car" driven by a former teacher. Cars were still rare and expensive at that time and drew much attention.

He was immediately fascinated by the university town. Some sights were strange and unexpected, such as the warm clothes many students wore in spite of the unusually hot fall season and

Exeter College, where Tolkien resided as a student, was the fourth oldest college in Oxford.
Tejvan Pettinger, Creative Commons

the long and narrow boats, called **punts**, they cruised up and down the River Cherwell, which runs through the city. To Tolkien, these boats, steered and propelled with a long pole, seemed as strange as camels.

But most of Oxford had an ancient charm. The majority of its buildings and traditions dated back to the Middle Ages—an era Tolkien had come to love. Exeter College, the specific school Tolkien was to attend, was founded in 1314. Tolkien knew he would get an excellent education. What he didn't know was that Oxford was going to be his home for most of his life.

His chosen course of studies, classics, covered Greek and Latin, including the history and philosophy of Ancient Greece and Rome. It was a five-year course that offered good prospects of a future career—in Tolkien's day, these subjects were still taught in high schools and considered indispensable in many fields.

To this basic course, he added a subject he had always found interesting: comparative philology, the study of the relationships between languages. He particularly wanted to know more about the languages that had most influenced modern English, to understand their roots and how they had evolved over time, with changes of spelling and even meaning. His teacher was Joseph Wright, a scholar Tolkien had already come to admire while he studied Gothic.

As was common in those days, Wright opened his home to Tolkien for private lessons. On Sunday afternoons, Joseph and his wife Elizabeth (also a philologist) would offer the young student tea and large slices of plum cake. During these visits, Tolkien was able to meet Wright's legendary Scottish terriers, Jack and Grendel (the latter named after a monster in *Beowulf*, an epic poem written in Old English). Apparently, Jack recognized the Gothic language and responded by sticking out his tongue. The word *smakka-hagma*, Gothic for "fig tree," made Jack lick his lips.

When Tolkien expressed his longstanding passion for Welsh—the language he had first seen on train trucks—Wright encouraged him to pursue it and to focus on the language of the early inhabitants of Wales: the Celts. Celtic history was a popular subject at that time and expertise on the topic promised to pay well. Tolkien chose medieval

A group of people punting on the River Cherwell near Oxford, England.
Sihasakprachum, iStock

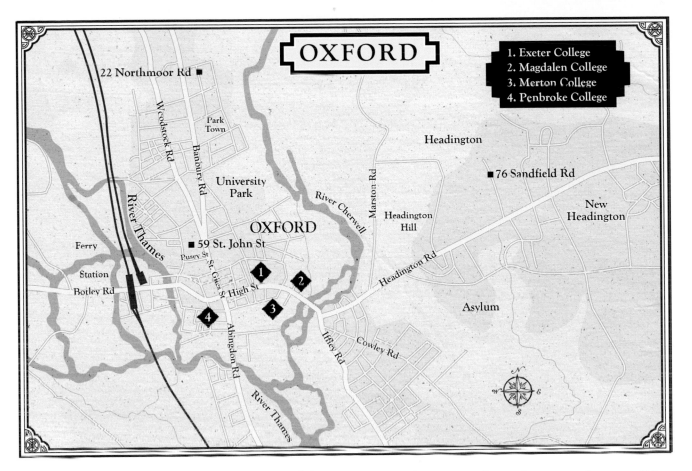

Welsh instead, simply because it was beautiful to his ears. Words were to Tolkien what colors are to artists or notes are to musicians. He appreciated their *beauty*, not only their meaning.

FELLOWSHIPS OLD AND NEW

What Tolkien missed most from King Edward's were his friends, especially a small group of young men who had worked with him in the school library. They had called their group the Tea Club, Barrovian Society (T.C.B.S.) after a nearby teashop (Barrow's Stores) where they spent hours talking about their dreams, ambitions, discoveries, and literary accomplishments.

After leaving King Edward's, he kept frequent correspondence with two of his T.C.B.S. mates, Christopher Wiseman and Robert Gilson (son of the school's principal), and became particularly close to another, Geoffrey (or G. B.) Smith, who transferred to Oxford in 1913.

Before Smith's arrival, though, Tolkien also made new friends at Oxford. This was not difficult. The university provided many clubs and activities, and Tolkien participated in so many that, according to the *King Edward's School Chronicle,* he seemed to have "joined all the Exeter societies which are in existence."

He also founded a new group called the Apolausticks (from the Greek *apolaustos,* meaning "enjoyable"): a group of young men who took turns hosting meetings in their rooms over food, drinks, and interesting conversations. By choosing that name, Tolkien might have wanted to emphasize the goal of the new society (having fun), or tried to play on the word "apostles," since its membership was limited to twelve—like the twelve apostles appointed by Jesus Christ. Later, he started another similar club, called Chequers Clubbe, but none of these could take the place of T.C.B.S.

Tolkien was able to rejoin the T.C.B.S. during his first Christmas vacation. Robert Gilson, then secretary of the musical and dramatic society for King Edward's School, invited the group to perform an 18th-century play—*The Rivals,* by Richard Brinsley Sheridan.

Tolkien played Mrs. Malaprop, a lady who had a funny habit of misusing words. It was an interesting part for someone like Tolkien, who enjoyed exploring language. After the dress rehearsal, the young men put on coats over their costumes and went for tea at Barrow's. Tolkien must have attracted some attention as he walked through downtown Birmingham in a woman's costume and makeup. In fact, all of Barrow's patrons must have been surprised when the actors took off their coats!

LOVE REKINDLED

If friends and societies occupied much of Tolkien's time, he never forgot Blatt. On January 3, 1913, he turned 21. This meant he was no longer under Father Francis's guardianship and was free to contact her. He wrote to her as the clock struck midnight, telling her that his feelings had not changed during the long months, almost three years, that they had been apart. He asked her to marry him.

What Tolkien Ate in College

Most of the time, Tolkien ate in the common hall with the other students. If he didn't want to do that, he could order food (especially breakfast) in his room. It was delivered by a servant, called a "scout," who was assigned to this specific duty. Sometimes, students ate breakfast together in someone's room, and they took turns paying for it.

Some of Tolkien's bills show some of the common food items he ordered. They included "**porridge**, eggs and buttered toast with honey, **marmalade**, jam or anchovy; crumpets, muffins, cakes, sardines; and potted meat. He was also charged for sauce, pickles, and **chutney**; for tea and coffee, milk and cream, lemon squash."

The special dinners he enjoyed with different societies were much more extravagant. For example, the Old Edwardians' seventh annual London Dinner, held at the Holborn Restaurant, included ten courses and coffee, and the menu from an equally elaborate Apolausticks dinner at the Randolph Hotel included **foie gras**, Parisian-style beef, Parmesan cheese **soufflé**, Peach Melba, and much more.

The wait for her answer must have seemed endless. When her letter arrived, it didn't bear good news. Thinking that Tolkien had forgotten her, she had become engaged to the brother of a schoolfriend. Her fiancé was kind, she said, and she could accept him as a husband.

Other men might have given up, but Tolkien was determined. Being acceptable was not the same as being the right husband—and Tolkien believed he was the latter. He traveled to Cheltenham and met Blatt at the station, then they talked, walking together to the outskirts of town and sitting under a bridge. He promised to work hard at his studies so he could get a good job and give her the comfortable life she had grown accustomed to leading in the spacious home of her wealthy relatives.

In the end, she agreed to marry him and break her former engagement, but asked him to keep everything secret for some time. He consented. He only made an exception for Father Francis, who had done so much for him.

The Father must have expected this to happen. Whatever his personal feelings, he was probably comforted by the fact that Blatt had accepted to leave the Church of England and join the Roman Catholic Church.

Edith eventually broke the news to her host family who, being firmly Anglican, asked her to find new lodgings. She then decided to rent a small house with a middle-aged cousin, Jennie Grove, a short, spirited lady, and Jennie's dog, Sam. The house was in Warwick, less than 50 miles (80 km) north of Oxford. There, Blatt began

to take instructions at the local Roman Catholic church.

All this came at great sacrifice. Her host family lived in a spacious house with servants, where Blatt could play their grand piano as much as she liked. Her musical talents were also appreciated at her Anglican church. Her decision to become Roman Catholic was mostly based on her love for Tolkien, because religion was very important to him.

As for Tolkien, he returned to Oxford with a new spring in his step and pursued his studies with renewed vigor. To ensure his maximum

The Medieval castle on Ethelfleda's Mound was one of the many sights Tolkien enjoyed when he visited Blatt in Warwick, a town still largely unspoiled by factories. His 1915 poem "Kortirion Among the Trees" was dedicated to Warwick. About a year later, in *The Book of Lost Tales*, he described Kortirion as the city in Tol Eressëa, the island of the Elves, where the queen lived on a hill very similar to Ethelfleda's Mound. Tolkien and Blatt punted down the River Avon, which flows in front of the castle.
DeFacto, Wikimedia Commons

Make a Batch of Marmalade

While jars of marmalade can be bought in stores, most British people believe that they are no substitute for homemade marmalade. Since oranges are a winter fruit, making marmalade is a perfect occasion for hanging around the warm stove and filling the house with a delightful smell. It can be time consuming, but it's certainly rewarding.

You will find many recipes for marmalade on the internet, as each cook tends to be loyal to his or her method. The recipe in this book is simple, for first-time marmalade makers. You can always perfect your art later!

ADULT SUPERVISION REQUIRED

YOU'LL NEED

* 3 organic oranges with seeds (Seville oranges—also known as sour oranges, or Naranj—are the best, but can be hard to find. Valencia oranges are a possible alternative. Organic are recommended because you will be eating the peels.)
* Cutting board
* Knife
* Food processor (optional)
* 3-quart pot (2.8 L)
* Citrus squeezer
* Small bowl
* Scissors
* Cheesecloth
* Cooking string
* 3 cups water (0.7 L)
* Stove
* Pinch of salt
* 3 cups sugar (0.7 L)
* Long wooden spoon
* Saucer
* 2 16-oz clean jars with lids
* 1 piece of toasted bread
* Butter (optional)

1. Wash the oranges.

2. Place them on the cutting board and cut them in half with the knife.

3. Squeeze them with the citrus squeezer and place the juice in the small bowl

4. Place the scooped-out orange peels on the cutting board and cut each one in half.

5. Take each half and cut it into small strips. (For a less traditional but safer method, you may slice the halves with the slicing blade of your food processor).

6. Place the sliced strips in the pot. Add the juice you have just squeezed.

7. Use the scissors to cut a piece of cheese-cloth about 8" by 8" (20 cm by 20 cm).

8. Cut a piece of string, about 12" long (30 cm).

9. Take the pulp and seeds that you have collected in the squeezer and place them in the middle of the cheesecloth.

10. Gather the corners of the cheesecloth together to make a small pouch. Make sure all the pulp and seeds are wrapped securely. Hold the pouch over the pot and squeeze gently so that any excess juice can drop into the pot.

11. Take the piece of string and tie it firmly around the pouch, making sure that all the pulp and seeds are securely under the string. Place it in the pot, on top of the sliced orange peels.

12. Pour 3 cups (0.7 L) of water in the pot.

13. Place the pot on the stove and bring it to a boil, then lower the flame and let it simmer for 30 minutes or until the slices look transparent.

14. Turn off the heat and let the pot sit for a while. You can even cover it and leave it overnight, as this will allow the pectin from the seeds to thicken the liquid. And it allows you to take a break, because the second phase will require about 45 minutes.

15. When you are ready for the second phase, put the saucer in the fridge or freezer to chill.

16. Pour the sugar in the pot with the orange mixture and stir well until thoroughly mixed.

17. Place the pot back on the stove, turn the heat to high, and bring the mixture back to a boil.

18. Reduce the heat to medium-low and stir with the wooden spoon for 30 minutes. Hold the spoon as high on the handle as possible to avoid getting hit by any splatters.

19. Take the chilled plate out and use the wooden spoon to drop a little mixture on it.

20. Place the plate back in the fridge for 2 to 3 minutes. Keep stirring the mixture in the meantime.

21. Check the drop of mixture you put on the plate by touching it gently. If the mixture wrinkles at your touch, the marmalade is ready. If not, put another clean saucer in the freezer, keep the mixture on the stove for 5–10 more minutes, then repeat steps 19–21 using the new chilled plate.

22. Once the marmalade is ready, turn off the stove, take the pot off the heat, and let the mixture cool off, then pour it gently into the jars. Since this marmalade will be kept in the fridge, you don't need to sterilize the jars. If later you decide to make a larger batch and store it outside of the fridge, you must ask an adult to sterilize the jars for you. (Look online for the method.)

23. Enjoy your marmalade on toast, with or without butter.

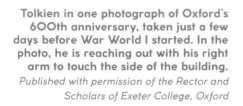

performance, he kept a journal where he marked the hours spent in his studies and in his religious activities.

Tolkien's commitment to his studies became easier when his classics tutor, Lewis Richard Farnell, who had been recently appointed as rector of the College, allowed him to change his academic course to English language and literature, facilitating the transition in such a way that it would not cause delays in Tolkien's studies. Finally, he could study exactly what he liked the most.

A DIFFICULT DECISION

As far as Tolkien could see, 1914 promised to be another good year. On January 8, Blatt was accepted into the Roman Catholic Church, and the two lovers officially announced their engagement.

Further, Tolkien was elected president of the Debating Society and received a £5 award for the Skeat Prize for English—which he used to buy a Welsh grammar book and three poetry books.

Feeling uplifted, Tolkien splurged on two new suits, new furniture, and some Japanese prints for his room. As soon as summer vacation started, he traveled to Warwick to spend time with Blatt.

Neither he nor any other student could have imagined what would happen next. On June 28, a young nationalist from Serbia shot Archduke Franz Ferdinand of Austria, the presumed heir of the Austro-Hungarian throne, and his wife, Sophia. This marked the start of World War I.

England entered the conflict on August 4 by declaring war on Germany. Three days later, the government issued an official call to arms to all able-bodied men.

As a university student, Tolkien had the choice to accept the call or finish his academic coursework, and he chose the second option. It was a bold decision, because society frowned on young

(left) **The assassination of Franz Ferdinand of Austria as it might have happened, illustrated by Achille Beltrame for the title page of the Italian newspaper** *Domenica del Corriere*, **1914.** *Wikimedia Commons*

(below) **In this 1914 picture, Tolkien stands in the middle of the second row from back for a photo with members of Exeter College's rugby and boat clubs. He was a member of the rugby club.** *Published with permission of the Rector and Scholars of Exeter College, Oxford*

A recruitment poster, urging women to encourage their men to go to war. *Wikimedia Commons*

men who delayed service to their country. Even walking down the street became dangerous for any man who didn't wear a proof of enlistment, because he could be punched or hit by overly zealous citizens.

In September, just before school reopened, Ronald visited Hilary and Aunt Jane in a farm the two comanaged. Like Ronald, Hilary had a passion for plants. Ronald discovered that most of his family shared in the common feelings toward recruitment. Hilary was getting ready to volunteer.

In spite of this, Ronald stood by his decision, mostly for practical reasons. He was still poor and had to think about his future in view of his upcoming marriage to Blatt. He had invested much time and effort in his studies. If he could just wait long enough to get his degree, he would have better chances of finding an appropriate position after the war.

In the meantime, he could continue to train with the Officers' Training Corps (OTC) at Oxford. Besides delaying his active duty, this would allow him to avoid the sneers of the people he met and to enter the war as an officer rather than a private, with the benefits that position allowed.

These practical concerns were in no way opposed to his love for England. He was deeply patriotic. In fact, his studies of Middle and Old English were largely motivated by a desire to discover and understand the origins of his country. But he also had a general dislike of war. In this particular situation, he felt uncomfortable fighting against Germany, the land of many of his ancestors.

At that time, many English people with German surnames were changing them because of the war. Even King George V changed his name from Saxe-Coburg-Gotha to the English Windsor. But Tolkien kept his. He believed he could love his British homeland without hating Germany. It was a noble and optimistic thought that was increasingly difficult to sustain in those emotionally charged days.

EÄRENDEL THE EVENING STAR

It was at his aunt's farm, around the end of the summer, that a ninth-century poem came back to Tolkien's mind—especially the first two lines: *Éala Éärendel engla beorhtast, ofer middangeard monnum sended!* ("Hail Eärendel, brightest of angels, above Middle-earth sent unto men!").

Strangely moved by these words, Tolkien decided to continue the story in a poem of his own: "The Voyage of Eärendel the Evening Star." He took only a few hints from the original poem. His poem was about a sailor who sailed off the earth into the sky as a bearer of light.

It was the beginning of a tale which stayed with Tolkien for the rest of his life—an initial seed that would later grow into his tales of Middle-earth—from *The Book of Lost Tales* to *The Lord of the Rings* (where the name became Eärendil, in the Elvish language of Quenya).

Rewrite an Ancient Tale

When Tolkien's friend G. B. Smith asked him what his Eärendel poem meant, Tolkien said he didn't know but was going to find out. That's because he thought stories are meant to be discovered rather than created. Anything—a word, a sound, or a sight—can grow into a story.

Storytellers can also find new ways of telling old tales by looking at them with new eyes, as if discovering them for the first time. Do you want to try to do the same?

YOU'LL NEED

❀ Paper

❀ Pen or pencil (or computer and printer)

1. Find a story from your heritage (from the country or countries of your ancestors). You may ask your family, search a library, or look online. Or you can just use any story you have enjoyed reading.

2. Read it as if you had never read it before. Try to see something new that you can tell others. For example, you can develop one smaller aspect of the story to become the focus or take one of the lesser characters in the story and try to imagine what his or her tale might have been. Think of yourself as discovering the story rather than creating it.

3. Put pen (or pencil) to paper and write out the new story you discovered.

4. Share your story with friends, family, or classmates.

4

WARTIME

B Y THE END OF THE summer, Oxford was a different place. War was now an ever-present reality. At Exeter, the number of students had been reduced to less than half, as most had signed up for military service. Some rooms were set up as temporary hospitals for wounded soldiers, who brought grim news from the warfront of **casualties** and defeats. The place was quiet, especially at night, when the few lit windows only made the darkness look more ominous.

French Red Cross workers in action on the Somme front.
National Photo Company Collection, Library of Congress

Rector Farnell allowed Tolkien to move out of the disheartening campus and rent a room in a nearby apartment with Colin Cullis, a close friend of Tolkien and member of the Apolausticks. Cullis had a heart condition which prevented him from joining the armed forces.

The apartment at 59 St. John's Street was close enough to the school for Tolkien to walk there in a matter of minutes but far enough to permit him to take his mind off the horrors of war.

In addition to classes, Tolkien and twenty-four other students attended daily drills at the OTC, for a total of six and a half hours per week—much less than the number of hours required from students who had enlisted. Tolkien found the schedule and exercises helpful to keep him alert and beat the sleepiness that often followed hours of intensive studies.

THE T.C.B.S. MEETS AGAIN

With the prospects of combat looming closer, Tolkien discussed with his friend Christopher Wiseman the need for a T.C.B.S. meeting. It was, in fact, overdue. Neither of them could find as much inspiration as they did when they were together. Tolkien believed "they had been granted some spark of fire . . . that was destined to kindle a new light." This sense of being a singular group with a unique mission spurred them on to greater things.

The date was set for December 12, 1914. The place was Wiseman's family home in London. There, the four remaining members of the group—Wiseman, Tolkien, Smith, and Gilson—sat around a gas fire, talking about their dreams, ambitions, and everything that made their group unique. Just a few hours together renewed their hopes, inspiration, and commitment to make this world a better place through art and writing. They called this meeting "the Council of London."

For Tolkien, this meeting marked a brand-new start, encouraging him to express things he had until then kept inside. His creative efforts became focused on the world he had been gradually describing. He wrote poems, painted sceneries of imaginary worlds, and developed the Elvish language he had previously invented: Quenya. For

Secondary World and Subcreation

Tolkien was ready to explain that, in his stories, he was not creating new worlds. He believed that God is the creator, and human beings are only subcreators. In fact, they subcreate precisely because they have inherited this ability from God. Subcreating is part of who they are.

For this reason, Tolkien called his subcreated world "secondary world." A writer's task is to make this secondary world believable—not because it's realistic, but because it makes sense within itself, according to its own laws. While you are in that world, you believe what you see and hear, even if much of it would never be seen or heard in our world.

Tolkien, producing a language for this world was essential in order to give a voice to his characters.

From a young age, he thought Britain lacked an organized collection of local myths, such as the Icelandic *Völsunga,* the Finnish *Kalevala,* or the myths of ancient Greece and Rome. England had the stories of King Arthur and his Knights of the Round Table, but they were told as set in a specific time. Tolkien was looking for tales which happened in a time not recorded in history, where imagination could roam free. Besides, the tales of King Arthur were written in a style that was closer to French traditional tales than to English ones. As many authors do, Tolkien saw a need and decided to meet it.

On September 25 and 26, 1915, the T.C.B.S. met one last time before the young men left for war. By that time, Wiseman had joined the Royal

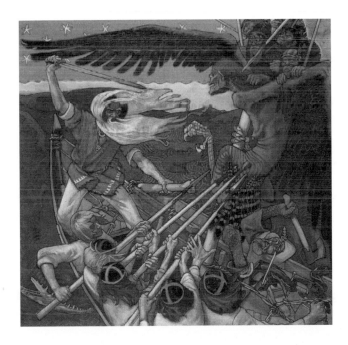

The Land of Faëry

One of Tolkien's first poems, "The Shores of Faëry" (1915), describes some of the worlds he had begun to explore, mentioning places he would later use in his books, such as Taniquetil, the holy mountain in Valinor.

But the word "fairy" had a different meaning for Tolkien than it has today. **Faëry,** in Old English, was a fantastic realm just beyond our world, which is home to creatures such as elves, dwarves, witches, giants, dragons, and—yes—fairies.

These creatures were nothing like the ones you see in modern cartoons. For example, fairies were powerful beings that could even be frightening, and elves were immortal and noble inhabitants of an ancient land.

Tolkien said that his love for Faëry didn't start when he was a child, even though he enjoyed fairy stories. It started later, when his love for old languages and his creation of new ones awakened a desire to know more about the people who may have been speaking them. This love came fully to life during the war, as a way to keep his mind occupied on better things.

An image from the Finnish saga *Kalevala,* painted by Finnish artist Akseli Gallen-Kallela. The hero Väinämöinen is seen wielding a sword to defend a precious artifact from the evil witch Loui.
HIP/Art Resource

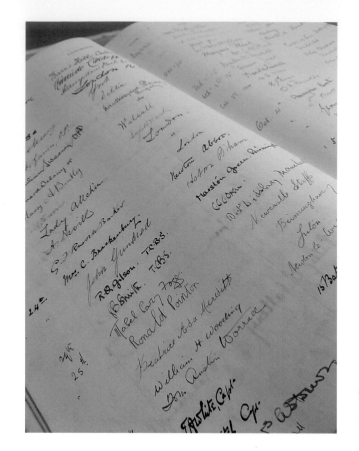

What they didn't know was that, on that very day, the German army killed thousands of men (most sources say 8,000) at the Battle of Loos, in France. Two of Tolkien's friends from the Apolausticks were among the dead. It was an omen of things to come.

LOVE AND WAR

Tolkien found military training boring, with its endless drills and lectures about weapons, map reading, hygiene, and rescue of fellow soldiers. He shared very few interests with the other officers and disliked the fact that the older officers treated him like a schoolboy. He had a moment of relief when he overheard another officer discussing a language he was inventing—someone else shared his passions after all.

Signaling was the only part of training that Tolkien found interesting, so he specialized in this field, learning how to transmit messages by flags, flashes of light, or sounds through different codes, such as Morse code.

By military regulation, soldiers could not disclose their location in any letters they sent during the war. But Tolkien and Blatt hatched the idea of developing a personal code, with which he could secretly tell her where he was when he wrote to her during his deployment. Blatt planned to keep a large map of France on her wall so she could follow Tolkien's travels.

Knowing he would soon leave for war, Tolkien and Blatt set a date for their wedding: March 22, 1916. They sent out invitations; the last was sent

Navy as an instructor in mathematics. Gilson was a second lieutenant in the army, and Smith, also in the army, had been promoted to full lieutenant.

Smith had encouraged Tolkien to apply for a commission in his unit, the 19th Battalion of a regiment known as the Lancashire Fusiliers, but the army placed Tolkien in the 13th Battalion instead—a reserve unit.

This meeting happened at the George Hotel in Lichfield, Staffordshire, near the camp in Brocton, where Tolkien was stationed. The young men were able to encourage one another one more time before leaving for war.

to Father Francis, because Tolkien was not sure how he would react. The priest replied with warm and heartfelt wishes, offering his services if they needed him to officiate the ceremony. It was too late, because Tolkien and Blatt had already asked Father Murphy of the church St. Mary Immaculate in Warwick, where Blatt had been attending. But Tolkien was happy to know that Father Francis was supportive.

After the ceremony, the newlyweds traveled to Clevedon, a quiet place in the county of Somerset, for a week's honeymoon. On the train, Edith practiced on the back of a telegram a few versions of her new signature: *Edith Tolkien, Edith Mary Tolkien, Mrs. Tolkien. . . .*

They took advantage of this trip to travel about 17 miles (27 km) south to one of Britain's most stunning views, Cheddar Gorge and Caves, with its limestone cliffs rising over 400 feet (120 m) and beautiful stalactite caves. Tolkien was greatly impressed. He later wrote that this memory inspired his description of the Glittering Caves of Aglarond, where many women, children, and elderly people found refuge in *The Lord of the Rings*.

After their honeymoon, Edith and her cousin Jennie moved from Warwick to the village of Great Haywood, about nine miles (14 km) north of Ronald's military camp. Ronald visited every time he could until his departure on June 4. The final goodbye was painful for the young couple, even though they had known it was coming. In fact, Tolkien said it was "like death," because they didn't know if they would ever see each other again.

The heliograph was one of the tools used by military signalers. It allowed them to communicate by Morse code through flashes of light. *Scanned by Signal Mirror, Flickr, from an Imperial War Museum photograph*

One of the caves at Cheddar Gorge. *Rob Stubbings*

Invent a New Code

In the Morse code, each letter of the alphabet and numerical digit correspond to a combination of dots and dashes. Ronald and Edith's system included only dots. They wrote their secret messages in the borders of a regular letter, so it looked like a decoration. Try something similar with one of your friends.

YOU'LL NEED

* 2 small pieces of paper (or a piece of paper and a card)
* Pen or pencil
* Morse Code Chart

1. On a piece of paper, write a simple message in Morse code. For example, "I love you." This is just to be used as a guideline.

2. Now think of different symbols you can use to disguise your message. For example, you can use flowers for dots and leaves for dashes. You can also use only dots, as Ronald and Edith did—maybe by making them of different sizes. But don't make your code too similar to Morse code, then the enemy might decipher it!

3. Write your message with the new symbols on the top and/or bottom of your second piece of paper (or card). Make it look like a decoration.

4. Write a nonsecret message (one that the enemy can see) on the main portion of the paper or card.

5. Explain your code to some of your trusted friends, then give them your message and see if they can decipher it.

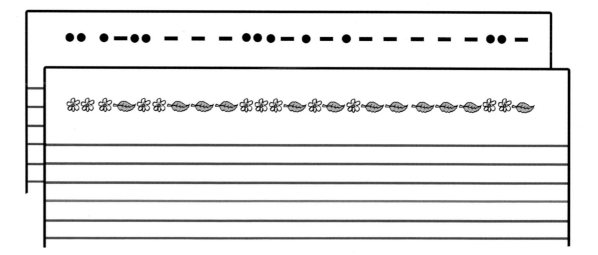

LIFE IN THE TRENCHES

Tolkien traveled by train to the port town Folkestone, in the county of Kent, where he and the men in his battalion boarded a ship to Calais, France. The crossing of the English Channel on June 6 was an emotional time for Tolkien, who wrote a farewell poem to his land, seeing it in all its beauty through his tears.

In France, Tolkien and his soldiers spent three weeks training at the British camp at Étaples, on the northern coast. There, he came to especially admire the private soldiers who served faithfully in spite of living in much poorer conditions than the officers. He was particularly impressed by his "batmen"—privates who were assigned to officers to act as their servants. Many years later, he still remembered them as "far superior" to himself. As an officer, he was not allowed to socialize with them, but he tried to help them as much as possible. Sometimes, during long marches, he carried the backpack of a soldier who was too tired to go on.

Before moving to the frontline, Tolkien was transferred from the 13th Battalion, which was a reserve unit, to the active 11th. On June 27, he and other men started the slow journey—first by train, then in a seemingly endless march—toward the Somme Valley.

The name Somme seems to come from the Celtic *samara*, meaning "calm." Tolkien, in his love for languages, would have known this. But on that day, the valley was anything but calm, shaken as it was by the noise of gunfire and grenades.

Tolkien learned quickly that the conditions of war were quite different from those he had experienced at the OTC and in the military camps at home. Here, much of the equipment was old and faulty, the sleeping arrangements were rough, and the sound of war was all too real.

World War I saw the rise of a new style of fighting called "trench warfare." A trench was a long, muddy row which an army dug in the ground to shield them from gunfire, roughly parallel to the enemy's trench. It was usually dug in a zigzag line, which was harder for the enemy to overrun.

Each trench was typically close enough to the enemy that officers in opposite camps could communicate with each other by yelling. The

Wounded British soldiers in a trench. *George Grantham Bain Collection, Library of Congress*

Make a Soldier's Staple Food

Since bread had to travel from camps where large ovens were available, it was often stale by the time it reached the soldiers. Even dry biscuits, which have a longer shelf life, could taste stale after months, especially if the packages were opened. Sometimes, the cooks would simply wet the bread and place it in an oven to revive it.

A more common solution was to use stale bread and biscuits for puddings. The following is a simple recipe for a bread pudding as they might have made it in a World War I military camp. Try it out for you and your family or friends (it feeds four people).

ADULT SUPERVISION REQUIRED

YOU'LL NEED

* Oven
* Medium mixing bowl
* 4 slices (or 1 cup/240 ml) of stale bread, broken into pieces
* ½ cup (120 ml) milk
* Small whisk or fork
* ½ cup (120 ml) sugar
* 2 heaping tablespoons of raisins (add more if you like, or use a combination of dry cranberries and raisins, or raisins and chopped nuts)
* cinnamon or allspice
* 1 egg
* Small bowl
* Butter
* 2 small, rectangular baking pans

1. Preheat oven at 350°F (180°C).
2. Place the bread in the mixing bowl and cover with milk. Leave it for about 10 minutes or until soggy.
3. Mash it with a whisk or fork.
4. Stir in the sugar, raisins, and spices.
5. Crack the egg into the smaller bowl and whisk it.
6. Add the egg to the bread mixture and stir to combine.
7. Coat the baking pan with butter.
8. Pour the bread mixture into the pan and place it in the oven.
9. Bake at 350°F (180°C) degrees for half an hour or until the edges are browned. A fork pierced through the center should come out moist but clean.
10. (Optional) Sprinkle some extra sugar on top and bake for 3–5 more minutes to brown the sugar.
11. Allow the pudding to cool.
12. Take the pudding out of the pan, slice it, and serve it. It can be eaten cold or warm.

Feel free to make substitutions. All of these ingredients were not always available, and the military cooks had to make do with what they had at hand. The milk they used was canned or powdered, mixed with water, but fresh milk is fine.

territory between two opposing trenches was called no-man's-land. Those who were wounded or died in that wretched strip would often lie there for days before someone could venture to pick up their bodies.

In rare occasions, soldiers would be ordered to "go over the top" for an all-out charge through no-man's-land into the enemy trench. Sometimes, an army would bombard a trench or fire chemical agents such as mustard gas. Because of this, the soldiers in trenches lived crouched down in a constant state of alarm, cold and often wet from rain or mud, with limited supplies and little sleep.

Tolkien survived the stress of war the way he handled many other challenges—by keeping his mind on better things and happier worlds. Whenever he could—in his tent by candlelight, in the army's cafeteria, during the long military lectures, and even in the trenches—he thought of languages and legends and wrote whatever he had time to write: poems, letters, diary entries, and notes about the legends he had been conveying. He jotted down stories of Melkor (or Morgoth), the Dark Lord and rebel angel who rose in pride but was eventually bound in chains and thrown into the Void. It might have served as a hope that evil, even the unconceivable evil of war, would one day be defeated.

THE BLOODIEST DAY AND ITS AFTERMATH

Both British officers and soldiers expected a victory during their July 1 attack against German

An exhausted soldier asleep in a trench.
National Library of Scotland

troops. After a week of heavy bombardments on the enemy's camp, they expected it to be pulverized. The roar of the last bombardment, at 7:28 AM on the same day, was so loud that it was heard in London.

During the last few moments before the attack, a battalion of British soldiers filled the air with a different sound: a cheery love song they sang as a reminder of their girlfriends at home and the victorious news they would soon send them. The attack was meant to be the breakthrough in the war against Germany.

In reality, the German defenses were not as damaged as the British forces imagined. With plenty of time to get ready, the Germans had built impregnable trenches, low in the ground and well protected by thick entanglements of barbed wire, and their hidden machine guns were ready to fire.

Press flowers

Corresponding with loved ones back home was a great comfort to soldiers at war. They wrote letters whenever they could, adding poems or drawings. Many sent pressed dry flowers to their women at home. Do the same for someone you love.

Note: Since at that time people still dipped their pens into inkwells, they had plenty of blotter sheets available and used those to press their flowers. Tissue paper (which they didn't have at the time) works just as well.

YOU'LL NEED

❋ 2 tissues (or 2 paper towels)

❋ A few books

❋ Extra weight (such as a dumbbell) if available

1. Fold the tissue or paper towel in half and place it inside a book.

2. Place your flower on top of the tissue. Arrange it in the way you want it to appear when dry.

3. Fold another tissue or paper towel and place it on top of the flower.

4. Gently close the book.

5. Place the book in a safe place where it will not be moved or opened.

6. Stack other books on top. If you have a weight, place that on top of the pile.

7. Leave the flower untouched for a week, then open and check it. If the flower is not dry, leave it for another week and check again. Some flowers take longer than others to dry.

8. Once it is dry, remove the flower from tissues and the book. Handle it carefully; they can be very fragile! Enclose the flower in a letter to someone you love.

If you enjoy this activity, you can dry more flowers and use them for bookmarks or greeting cards by gluing then on cardboard and covering them with contact paper. Or you can ask an adult to help you set them in Epoxy resin; instructions can be found online or in many craft books.

Less prepared, the hopeful British who ventured out of their trenches at their officer's whistle call were mowed down by a flurry of bullets before they knew what was happening. In just one day, later described as "the bloodiest day in military British history," 19,240 British men were killed, 35,493 wounded, and 2,152 missing.

On that day, the 11th Battalion stayed as reserve at the nearby village of Bouzincourt. His life was spared, but he couldn't escape the horrors of the battle as the sounds, sights, and smells of the ghastly carnage invaded his camp. The silence that followed was even more ominous, signifying the end of thousands of lives and the stifling of the beleaguered British soldiers' common dream.

Tolkien feared for Gilson and Smith, who had been in the thick of the battle. He was filled with relief when, on July 6, Smith showed up at Bouzincourt, safe after 60 hours of intense gunfire, and was able to stay for a few days. Neither had heard anything about Gilson, but they were hoping for the best.

Smith's visit gave the two young men a few chances to talk and enjoy each other's company, discussing poetry and war and encouraging each other with the reminder that what was around them was not all there was to life. Later, Tolkien remembered an image from their walks together that seemed to confirm their hopes: a field of poppies, waving in the wind in spite of the engulfing desolation all around.

The battle continued for four long months, with Tolkien's battalion moving to the trench for a time on July 14 and then again on July 24. Their march to the front was like a nightmare, surrounded as they were by corpses no one had time to collect.

As a signaler, Tolkien had the duty of maintaining communication between the front lines and the rear, as well as communicating with headquarters. The tasks were frustrating. When he arrived at the communication center, he found that many of the systems he had learned could not be used. The Germans had tapped the telephones and were close enough to hear Morse signals and see light flashes.

Besides, the map of the area that he had carefully drawn turned out to be seriously flawed, based on false accounts given by German prisoners of war. Meanwhile, the German forces had had months to study the area and connect telephone wires to their bunkers and trenches.

Between attacks, Tolkien received a heartbreaking letter from Smith: Gilson had died during the July 1 attack, but his body wasn't recovered until days later. Smith felt crushed. This was more than a loss of a dear friend—as painful as such a loss always is. The T.C.B.S. had become such an intimate fellowship that losing Gilson was like losing a part of one's body. Both Smith and Tolkien spent a few sleepless nights thinking about their friend.

Tolkien had the hopeless feeling that the T.C.B.S. had ended. But Smith disagreed. He felt that the group represented something deeper than the physical presence of its members, and it would continue even if only one person was left to carry the torch.

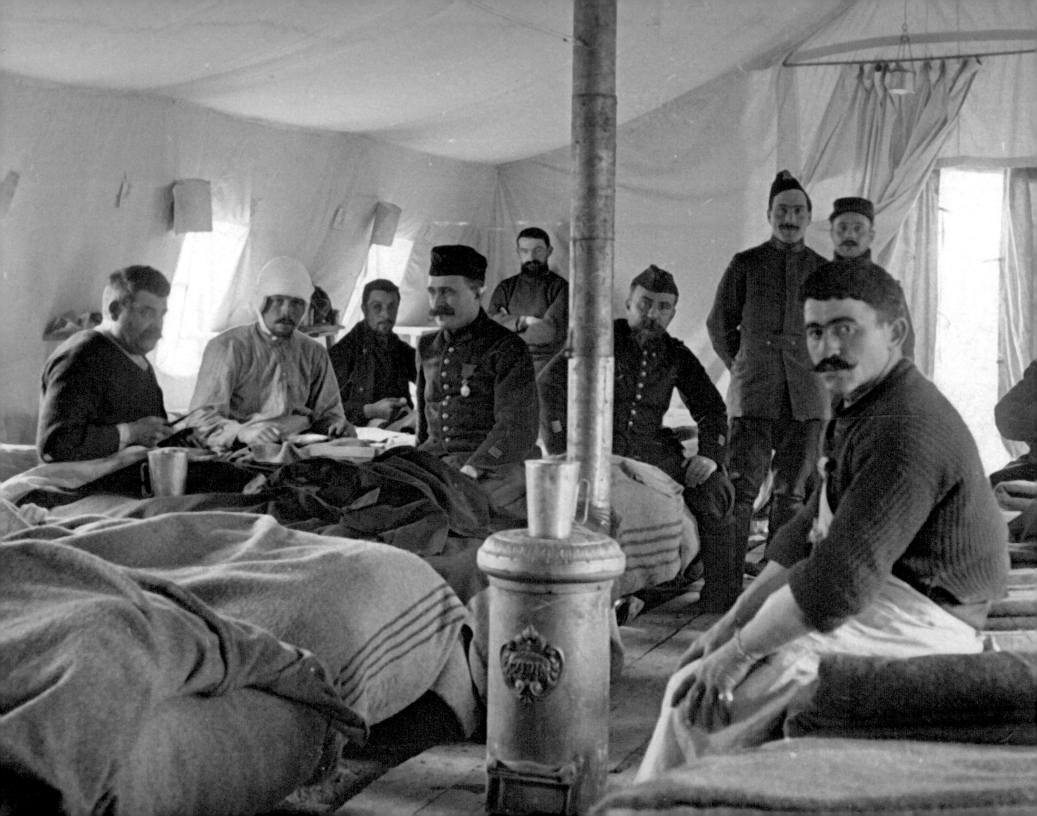

5

LOST TALES FOUND

BY THE END OF 1916, those who had hoped for a quick and victorious war for Britain were deeply disappointed. The conflict continued with many losses and little relief in sight, as the enemy was better equipped and prepared than the British had predicted.

Injured soldiers in a tent that served as a hospital near the Somme, France.
Sheldon Marshall, Art Resource

Tolkien was saved from long-term deployment by a serious bout of "trench fever," a bacterial disease. The bacteria were most likely carried by lice—a common problem among soldiers who lived in close quarters with little time to bathe. Once this was discovered, the army ordered the soldiers to bathe at least every two weeks.

Since antibiotics did not yet exist, the common treatment for trench fever was rest. But this fever was a recurrent illness; a soldier could feel better for a while and then relapse. What's more, a fever that lasted a long time or was combined with other diseases or injuries could lead to death.

Tolkien's fever struck on October 27, 1916. He was initially admitted to the local officers' hospital, then transferred to a facility at Le Touquet, and eventually to Le Havre, near the English Channel, with the intention of transferring back to England. On November 8, he was sent to Birmingham, in a temporary hospital inside the university. He was later assigned to a reserve battalion of the Lancashire Fusiliers at Thirtle Bridge, a camp on the east coast of England, about 150 miles (240 km) northeast of Birmingham. Since the army gave him leave until January 1917, he spent as much time as he could with Edith, who moved in order to be closer to him.

ONE MORE LOSS, ONE MORE DRIVE

Edith's presence must have been particularly comforting when, ten days later, Ronald received more shattering news: a letter from Christopher Wiseman, telling him that G. B. Smith had died of gangrene from a wound in his right arm.

Immediately, Tolkien wrote to Smith's mother to express his condolences and to report some accounts of her son's last months in France. She was now one of the many grieving mothers of this dreadful war. She asked Tolkien if he had any of her son's poems and expressed her desire to get them published.

Wiseman thought that publishing Smith's poems would be a good project for the T.C.B.S.—a way to keep the legacy alive. Tolkien agreed, and the two worked as coeditors, while a former teacher helped them to find a publisher. Two years later, the book was printed under the title *A Spring Harvest*.

In the meantime, the bedrest gave Tolkien time to do some writing of his own, an endeavor that became more urgent now that only he and Wiseman were left to carry on the T.C.B.S. vision. Wiseman encouraged Tolkien to start the epic he had always wanted to write.

THE BIRTH OF MIDDLE-EARTH

Soon, the epic started to take shape. The stories that had been twirling in Tolkien's mind for years, finding occasional expression in short tales, poems, and watercolors, flowed from his pen with renewed vigor.

Later, he gathered these stories in a collection he called *The Book of Lost Tales*. It was his first considerable work of fantasy, including myths on the origin of Elves, Dwarves, and Orcs and a description of the locations in which these stories are set, such as Middle-earth and Valinor, a land beyond the western ocean.

One of the first of these tales, "The Cottage of Lost Play," tells the story of a traveler, Eriol, who arrives at the Lonely Isle of Tol Eressëa, off the coast of Valinor. There, some Gnomes (a race of Elves) tell him the long history of Middle-earth. Tolkien explained that Tol Eressëa was really England at a time long gone, before any of its known early inhabitants (such as the Anglos and the Saxons) had arrived.

In fact, Tolkien went even further back in time, imagining that Ilúvatar (the creator of all things) sang angelic creatures named Ainur into existence and taught them how to make music so that their compositions would always be unique yet in harmony with each other.

This harmony was disrupted when the rebel Melkor blasted his clashing tunes, promoting, for the first time, pride, hate, and destruction. Far from being defeated, Ilúvatar was able to use these hostile sounds to create a more profound music. In fact, the notes of "immeasurable sorrow" the struggle produced turned out to be its chief source of beauty. When Melkor's opposition increased, "it seemed that its most triumphant notes were taken by the other and woven into its own solemn pattern."

Once the battle of the tunes ceased, Ilúvatar reminded Melkor that the evil he had created would, in the end, contribute to Illúvatar's glory and "make the theme more worth the hearing, Life more worth the living, and the World so much the more wonderful and marvellous."

Tolkien's Inspiration

While it's true that Tolkien drew much inspiration from the ancient tales of northern Europe and the British Islands (including the exciting tales passed down by the Celts, the inhabitants of much of ancient Europe), these were not his only source in the subcreation of his worlds.

According to scholar John Garth, he was also inspired by the Greek and Roman classics he read from a very young age, by the art and architecture of the Byzantine Empire (the eastern part of the Roman Empire that persisted after the fall of Rome), by ancient tales of the Assyrian Empire, and even by African tales and American poems. Henry Wadsworth Longfellow's *The Song of Hiawatha*, for example, sparked Tolkien's interest in Native American legends and languages.

We can find these influences in his writings, not as a collage or patchwork of stories and thoughts, but as a perfect blend, in which the individual ingredients are hardly noticeable.

And so it was that, while the Ainur played their music, even if flawed, the world came into being, where the music would continue to echo and the Sons of Men would continue to unconsciously desire it, until the day when harmony would once again reign unopposed.

Most of Tolkien's tales describe this battle between good and evil. On the good side, under Ilúvatar, are the Elves and other creatures, such as the Ainur, Valar, and Maiar. On the evil side, there is Melkor and a host of Orcs and Balrogs (fiery creatures armed with whips or swords).

Tolkien wrote these stories in pencil, which was easy to correct, until he was satisfied with them. Then he rewrote them in ink, sometimes over the original pencil. Sometimes Edith took over this final step. Most likely, she helped Ronald in other ways, too, such as editing and advising.

Edith was also the inspiration for some of his stories. One in particular, "The Tale of Tinúviel," was inspired by a walk Ronald and Edith took into the woods near Roos, Yorkshire, about a mile from the place where Ronald was stationed. Deep within these woods, the couple found a clearing filled with hemlocks. It was early summer, and the chestnut trees were also blooming with clusters of white and pink blossoms. Among the leaves, white moths were fluttering around, giving the place a fairytale appearance.

Inspired by these magical surroundings, Edith started to dance, her dark black hair contrasting the pale colors of the flowers and moths. And she was an excellent dancer. For Ronald, this was the beginning of a new story. He imagined a warrior, Beren, meeting the Elven princess Lúthien Tinúviel as she dances in the woods. Beren is immediately enchanted, and once he loses sight of her, he goes on a quest to find her.

Tolkien included this story in *The Book of Lost Tales*. Later, he developed it into a longer, adventurous story in a collection called *The Silmarillion*.

CARING FOR A GROWING FAMILY

Tolkien continued to report, from time to time, to the army's medical board. Though his health was improving, he was still weak, with occasional bouts of fever, and each examination found him unfit for any form of active service.

It was during one of these regular, mandatory examinations, on November 16, 1917, that Ronald received news that Edith had given birth to their first child, John Francis Reuel Tolkien. She had moved back to Cheltenham for the latter months of her pregnancy, where she had friends and family who could help her.

It was Ronald's aunt Mary who gave him the news. In spite of a difficult delivery, mother and baby were doing well. Ronald could not leave his post immediately, but he joined his family six days

A woodland glade filled with hemlocks in Yorkshire. *Michael Flowers*

Paint an Enchanted Forest

Use your imagination to paint the scenery Tolkien found in the woods near Roos. Use a small candle to mark the flowers and moths, which will appear white when you paint over them.

YOU'LL NEED

* Sheet of drawing paper
* Newspaper or plastic tablecloth (optional)
* Pencil
* Eraser
* Paints (any type)
* Paintbrushes
* Painter's palette or paper plate
* 1 cup (240 ml) of water
* Small birthday candle

1. Place the drawing paper on a clean surface (covered with newspaper or plastic tablecloth to catch paint spills, if needed).

2. Using a pencil, draw a row of trees (the leaves can just look like large clouds). Draw some grass by the tree roots.

3. Line up your paints, paintbrushes, palette, and cup of water. Keep the cup away from the paper to avoid spills.

4. Use the candle as a pencil to draw clusters of dots on the trees and on the ground, representing the flowers. With the same candle, draw a few more dots here and there to represent the moths. Don't worry if they are invisible. After you start painting in the steps to follow, the spots you have marked with the candle will look white.

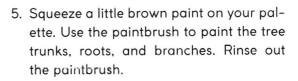

5. Squeeze a little brown paint on your palette. Use the paintbrush to paint the tree trunks, roots, and branches. Rinse out the paintbrush.

6. Squeeze some green paint on your palette. Paint the leaves on the trees and the grass on the ground. If you like, you can add some yellow to the green when you paint the grass. Rinse out the paintbrush.

7. Squeeze some light blue paint on your palette. Paint the spaces between the trees blue.

8. Let the painting dry.

later for the baby's baptism. To pay for the medical expenses related to the birth, he had to sell the last of the shares in South African mines, which he had inherited from his mother.

Ronald knew he was going to need more money to support his growing family and was glad when, in October 1918, the medical board declared him fit enough to hold a sedentary job. His first thought went back to Oxford, a place he had grown to love, even though his hopes of been employed there were slim. Though he was talented and well educated, he was still only a recent graduate.

An opportunity came when William Craigie, his former tutor in Old Icelandic, asked him to join the staff that was working on a new English dictionary (today known as *The Oxford English Dictionary*). The project—started back in 1879—was almost complete. Tolkien was assigned to words starting with the letter *w*, beginning with *waggle*.

Besides listing the definitions and origins of every word, he had to research similar words in other languages, compile a list of references, write his findings on small slips of papers, and give them to the head of his team. Most of the words starting with a *w* are challenging, because they don't usually derive from Latin and Greek. The most puzzling was *walrus*. Today, the Bodleian Library of the University of Oxford still holds a copy of a notebook with a long list—in Tolkien's handwriting—of possible definitions and origins of the word. (You may visit your local library to see a copy of the Oxford English Dictionary, and to check the word *walrus* and other entries Tolkien compiled, including *warm*, *wasp*, *water*, *wick*, *wallop*, *winter*, and of course, *waggle*).

The dictionary work was perfect for someone who loved languages as much as Tolkien did. The dictionary's editor was impressed by Tolkien's knowledge and abilities, especially since, at 25, Tolkien was still relatively young. Tolkien and his editor respected each other, even if they didn't agree on the etymology of every word. By the end, Tolkien said he had learned more during that time than during any other equal period in his life.

William Craigie.
*Special Collections Research Center,
University of Chicago Library*

A view of Leeds, taken in 1885, about 40 years before Tolkien lived there.
By kind permission of Leeds Libraries, www.leodis.net

Furthermore, the job came at the perfect time. On November 11, 1918, Tolkien heard the joyful news that an armistice had been signed, ending the war on land, air, and sea. He was now free to fully devote his time to his work without fear of being called back into active service.

BUILDING A HOME

To make ends meet, Tolkien supplemented his dictionary work with tutoring. Many of his students came from women's colleges. At that time, most tutors were young men who had just graduated from college and did not yet hold a permanent position. But having a young man tutor a young woman, particularly alone, was considered inappropriate. Being married, Ronald had the advantage of being able to tutor in his home, where Edith's presence made the young women feel at ease.

By the late summer of 1919, he was earning enough money to move his family to a small rented house on what is now called Pusey Street. One of John's early memories of that home was elephants walking by daily during the the annual St. Giles' Fair, where they were exhibited along with other animals. The elephants were so large that, when they passed by the Tolkiens' home, they blocked the light from the dining room window.

The house was spacious enough to hold Edith's piano, which had been left in storage while the Tolkiens lived in smaller lodgings. Edith was also able to hire a helper who could do some cooking and cleaning. Edith's older cousin Jennie Grove still lived with them and by this time had become a substitute mother for Edith and a grandmother figure for John, who called her Aunt Ie. She stayed with the family until 1921, when the Tolkiens moved to Leeds, about 170 miles (270 km) north of Oxford.

Leeds was not a choice location for someone who loved nature as much as Tolkien did. It was an industrial city, with so much pollution that the smoke left its mark on clothes and the chemicals in the air made the curtains rot.

But Tolkien had to work there in order to give his family a more comfortable life. He started out as reader of English at the University of Leeds.

The Industrial Revolution

The Industrial Revolution began in England in the 18th century. It marked a period of transformation from an agricultural economy to an industrial one. Products that used to be made by artisans became manufactured in great quantities.

The Industrial Revolution brought more people to the cities. This caused the cities to become overcrowded and increased poverty for those who couldn't find work. Pollution was another problem. Industries depended almost entirely on coal as a source of fuel, and the constant burning of coal polluted the air.

Tolkien's house at 2 Darnley Road in Leeds.
Sagarjethani, Wikimedia Commons

In 1924, he was promoted to professor. With the promotion came a higher salary—so much higher that Tolkien was able to buy a house surrounded by open fields, where he could take the children for walks.

Even Leeds would not be a permanent home, though. Tolkien enjoyed his new job and got along well with the head of his department, but when he learned about a vacant position at Oxford as professor of Anglo-Saxon, he applied. He was not nurturing high hopes; after all, he was young and still had limited experience. One month later, however, he received a letter from the college: he had been chosen for the prestigious job!

He moved to Oxford in 1925, and his family joined him the following year. By then, they had three boys: John, Michael, born in 1920, and Christopher, who was born in 1924 and named after Christopher Wiseman.

Edith was glad to move away from the pollution. And the family had suffered many problems since they moved to Leeds: Edith and the boys got measles, Michael had appendicitis, Ronald came close to death from pneumonia, and the house was robbed by thieves—apparently with the help of the maid. The Tolkiens were ready for a new start.

DAD, THE STORYTELLER

The family celebrated their move with a three-week vacation at Filey, a small town by the west coast of England. They stayed at a cottage on a cliff overlooking the sea. Ronald taught the children to skim stones on the water. The only setback was Michael, who was almost five, losing his favorite **porcelain** toy dog. Ronald and the boys looked for it for two days, but never found it.

A few days later, when a storm shook the house so violently that the roof seemed ready to fly away, Ronald calmed the frightened children by telling them a story. The subject? A dog named Rover who was turned into a porcelain dog by a wizard. The wizard renamed the dog Roverandom, then gave him to "Little Boy Two," a reference to Michael.

To become a real dog again, Rover had to find the wizard. That's why he escaped from the boy's pocket. Rover's adventures took him along the moon's silvery path up to the moon itself and then down under the sea, where he disturbed a sea serpent, provoking a storm. Along the way, Rover met many interesting characters. The story ended happily, helping to ease the boys' minds about the upsetting parts of their vacation.

This was not the first story Tolkien told his children, and it would not to be the last. Today, however, only a few of these stories are known— the ones he wrote down. One of these was *Farmer Giles of Ham*, which Tolkien improvised for the children when the family, caught in a sudden rainstorm after a picnic, had to find refuge under a bridge.

Famer Giles, Tolkien told them, was awakened by his dog to find that a giant was approaching. Ingeniously, Giles filled his gun with nails and shot the giant, who ran away, thinking he was being attacked by bees. Giles was rewarded by the king, who gave him a sword named Tailbiter, a famous slayer of dragons.

Later, when a dragon attacked the town, the people immediately thought of Giles and his sword. The farmer was once again victorious and, after a twist of events, became king.

Tolkien took every opportunity to stimulate the children's imagination and fill their lives with magic. According to some sources, Christopher's toy car with a rider inspired Tolkien's *Mr. Bliss*, a children's story about a man who faces incredible adventures during his first ride in his new motorcar, including an encounter with bears—likely inspired by the Tolkien boys' teddy bears.

At Christmas, when many parents encourage their children to write letters to Santa Claus, Tolkien went one step further. He wrote letters *to* the children, as if Father Christmas (as Santa was known in England) were the author. He started this tradition in 1920, when John was three years

The full moon rising over the sea at Filey. From their rented cottage, the Tolkien family enjoyed a similar view, with the moonlight drawing a silvery path on the water. *Mark Richards*

Write a Letter from Father Christmas

Pretend you are Father Christmas and write a letter from his perspective to someone you know (your parents, a sibling, a relative, or a friend). Let your imagination run freely as you describe other characters, events, situations, and feelings. Add pictures to both the letter and the envelope.

YOU'LL NEED

- ❅ 2 sheets of paper
- ❅ Pencil
- ❅ Colored pencils, markers, or crayons
- ❅ Envelope
- ❅ Ruler

1. On a sheet of paper, write a letter from Father Christmas to someone you know. Try to use your best handwriting. You may draw and color some pictures if you like.

2. Write the address of the person to whom you are sending the letter on an envelope.

3. Use the ruler and pencil to draw a small rectangle, about 1.5 inches by 1 inch (4 cm by 2.5 cm), on the other sheet of paper.

4. Inside the rectangle, draw and color a small picture related to Christmas or winter. Add the words NORTH POLE and the year.

5. Use scissors to cut out the rectangle.

6. Glue the rectangle onto your envelope where the stamp would normally be.

7. Use a pencil to draw some lines on the envelope and stamp, where the post office would normally place their postmark. Write POLAR POSTAL SERVICE or something similar and the date.

8. Find a way to deliver it to your addressee. Be creative. Think of a method Father Christmas might use.

   If Christmas is still a long way, you can write a letter from the Tooth Fairy or any other mysterious being that might visit humans.

old, and continued for 20 years, until all his children were grown.

Sometimes, Tolkien made Father Christmas's experiences match a situation his family was facing or was about to face. For example, during Christmas 1925, when the family was about to move from Leeds to Oxford, Tolkien wrote an apology from Father Christmas to the children for writing only one letter instead of two. The reason? He had been busy moving to a new house, after the old one was accidentally damaged by his assistant, the clumsy North Polar Bear. He included the details of the accident and the bear's reaction.

With time, Tolkien began to write on behalf of other North Pole residents: the North Polar Bear (who continued to have accidents and cause delays), the bear's nephews Paksu and Valkotukka, Father Christmas's secretary (the elf Ibereth), snow-elves, red gnomes, snow-men, and other bears.

The letters were written in colored ink and included drawings and paintings. They arrived in envelopes sprinkled with snow and bearing artfully painted North Pole postage stamps. Sometimes, Tolkien left them by the fireplace, where the children placed their letters to Father Christmas. Carefully placed wet footprints made Tolkien's impersonation more credible. Other times, he asked the postman to deliver the letters.

SHARING LOVE FOR ART AND NATURE

On January 7, 1926, the Tolkiens moved into a house at 22 Northmoor Road, in North Oxford, about a mile away from where they previously lived and two miles from Penbroke College, where he worked. Every day, Tolkien covered that distance rapidly on his high-seated bicycle, dressed in the typical cap and gown British college professors wore in their classrooms.

But this home became too small when, in June 1929, the Tolkiens welcomed their fourth child, Priscilla Mary Anne Reuel Tolkien, into this world. Fortunately, about six months later, the larger house next door became vacant, and the family settled there.

Their new home had a good-sized yard that Tolkien redesigned to meet the family's needs. To do so, he enlisted the help of his son John,

The house at 20 Northmoor Road, Oxford, where the Tolkiens moved after the birth of Priscilla. *Michael Paetzold, Lizenz: https://creativecommons.org /licenses/by-sa/3.0/de/legalcode*

The fruitful Vale of Evesham, where Ronald's brother Hilary lived. *Jason Ballard, Creative Commons License*

passing on to him his love for plants in the process. Together, father and son built a wooden frame in front of the house, which served both as support for climbing plants and as a fence to protect the garden and keep it private. The garden was particularly beautiful in the spring, when many of the plants, such as daffodils and plum trees, were in flower.

The yard also included an aviary, where Edith kept canaries, budgerigars, and other exotic birds, as well as a tennis court, part of which Tolkien and his sons turned into a vegetable garden.

As usual, Tolkien took his children out for walks as often as possible, either all together or one at a time. During these walks, they often chased butterflies and looked closely at trees and plants. Sometimes, he took them punting on the River Cherwell, as he had learned to do in his first year as a student at Oxford.

During the summer, they went to the seaside, where they enjoyed swimming, shopping, playing clock golf (similar to minigolf), and collecting rare shells. As he had when he was young, Tolkien sketched or painted the sights that impressed him most. The memories of his youth became especially vivid in 1928, when Father Francis joined the family on their vacation at Lyme Regis. These seaside vacations inspired Tolkien to compose a collection of humorous poems for children, *Tales and Songs of Bimble Bay*.

Tolkien also took his family on frequent visits to his brother Hilary and some of Mabel's relatives in the Vale of Evesham, especially after 1932, when Ronald bought his first car—a Morris Cowley he nicknamed "Jo." Hilary had a fruit farm at Evesham, and John spent some of his yearly vacation time helping him to pick plums.

Each day, Tolkien spent many hours in his study, and his children, who found the place particularly exciting, were welcome to join him, unless he was tutoring.

Priscilla said it was only when she became an adult that she realized how hard her father worked. At the college, he gave more lectures than any of his colleagues. At home, besides tutoring, he graded papers for several universities. He had to do all this in order to meet his family's expenses and give them a comfortable life. The reason he could still spend time with his children is that he did much of his work (including his writing) at night so much that his friends wondered whether he got any sleep.

The main piece of furniture in Tolkien's study was his desk. On top of his desk, he kept his large stationery, which included bottles of ink of different colors, paints, colored pencils, and—later on—chalks. For Tolkien, drawing, coloring, and painting was an important part of his writing process, because it helped him to visualize some elements of the story, such as locations. In fact, his journey into his secondary world had begun with drawings as much as with words.

Tolkien's study included so many books that the shelves covered the walls completely, from floor to ceiling. There was also a black stove where he burned wood to keep warm. He would light it in the morning, but then he usually became distracted by his work and didn't tend to the fire until the neighbors or a postman warned him about the black smoke coming out of the chimney. This happened nearly every day.

Once, however, Tolkien received a more frightening warning. He was at the college, waiting to give an important speech, when a messenger told him his house was on fire! Thankfully, the fire, which had started in the loft, caused minimal damage, because Edith saw it in time and was able to put it out.

But the fire could have been disastrous in more ways than one. Besides the danger it posed to the family and their properties, it could have destroyed the countless pages of Ronald's writings, which, in these days without computers and photocopy machines, were rarely copied.

6

THERE LIVED A HOBBIT

AMONG THE PRECIOUS papers the fire left untouched was the start of a new story, *The Hobbit*. This story started almost by chance. Tolkien was correcting some exam papers—a busy task which required much concentration. He turned over a sheet and discovered that a student had left a blank page. He wrote in the blank space, quite absentmindedly, "In a hole in the ground lived a hobbit." He didn't know what a hobbit was, but decided he would eventually find out.

Bilbo's encounter with Smaug, as imagined by artist Ted Nasmith.
Ted Nasmith

Priscilla Tolkien holding the original drawing of Bilbo's hobbit-hole. She is looking at an enlargement of a stamp issued by the British Royal Mail in 2004 in commemoration of the 50th anniversary of the first two parts of *The Lord of The Rings. Topfoto*

The story evolved as he told it to his boys during their evening story time, when the family gathered by the fire and Tolkien sat in front of them, his back to the fireplace.

The boys were attentive listeners, especially five-year-old Christopher, who noticed every small detail, such as the color of a door, and corrected his father if, in the course of the story, anything was inconsistent.

As annoying as these corrections might have been at the time, Tolkien made note of them. Years later, when *The Hobbit* went to print, he paid Christopher two pence for every mistake he could find in the final draft. At that time, two pence could buy a candy bar or a comic book or could be saved for bigger purchases.

The Hobbit is a lighthearted adventure of a reluctant hobbit named Bilbo Baggins who lives in a region of Middle-earth called the Shire, in a home called Bag End—an English translation of the common French **cul-de-sac**. Like most hobbits, Bilbo enjoys his quiet, comfortable life and has no intention to change it. That is, until a wizard named Gandalf comes to turn it upside down.

Gandalf sends Bilbo along with thirteen dwarves to recover a treasure stolen by Smaug, the greatest fire-breathing dragon of the Third Age. On the way, Bilbo meets a slimy underground creature named Gollum, who has just lost a magical ring that makes its wearer invisible. Bilbo finds the Ring and takes it.

After many adventures fighting Trolls, wolves, and spiders with the assistance of Elves and eagles, Bilbo finds the dragon laying on its massive, stolen

We don't know how Tolkien came up with that word. It was, in fact, rather unknown. It was mentioned once in a 19th-century collection of popular stories, as one of many fantastic beings, which the author called spirits. But for Tolkien, a hobbit was not a spirit at all. It was just a small creature with furry feet.

Tolkien might have been thinking of the Old English *holbytla*, meaning "hole builder." His Hobbits did live in holes in the ground. But these holes were nothing like the dark tunnels an animal might build. They were comfortable places, with all the commodities an upper-class Englishman living in Tolkien's time would wish to have, including well-stocked pantries, fireplaces, and featherbeds.

Eventually, once he had decided what Hobbits were, Tolkien weaved a story about one of them.

treasure and discovers a vulnerable spot between its scales. This allows the warrior Bard, a descendent of Girion, Lord of Dale, to kill the dragon and recover the treasure. In the end, Bilbo returns a changed hobbit to his restful hole in the ground.

A FAITHFUL FRIEND

In 1933, Tolkien lent an unfinished copy of his story to another professor at Oxford, his friend Clive Staples Lewis, commonly known as C. S. Lewis (but his friends called him Jack).

Lewis and Tolkien first met in 1926. They didn't immediately become best friends. In fact, initially they disagreed on an item in the Oxford English School curriculum: the separation between studies of language and studies of literature. Tolkien thought that language and literature should be taught together, because they complemented each other. He also thought the English curriculum should include a study of both ancient and medieval English, as well as texts written in those languages. Lewis disagreed. With time, however, he came to believe that Tolkien was right.

It took some time for Lewis to warm up to Tolkien. Growing up in a Protestant home, he had been told not to trust Roman Catholics. As an English professor, he had also come to distrust philologists. And Tolkien was both.

Lewis was, however, interested in a club Tolkien had started for the purpose of reading and translating Old Icelandic sagas. The club's

Magdalen College.
Ed Webster, Creative Commons license

Create Your Version of the Necklace of Girion

The Necklace of Girion was just one of the magnificent objects that appear in The Hobbit. *This piece of jewelry, adorned with 500 emeralds, was originally owned by Girion, Lord of Dale, who gave it to the Dwarves of Erebor in exchange for a coat of Dwarf-linked rings for his eldest son. The coat was made with a type of pure silver that was three times as strong as steel—a great means of protection in war.*

When the dragon Smaug attacked Dale and Erebor, he took the necklace as part of the spoils. But he was soon defeated and killed. The necklace was assigned to Bard, the heir of Girion, who in turn gave the emeralds to the Elvenking as a gesture of gratitude.

You can create your own version of the Necklace of Girion—not as precious, but equally empowering.

YOU'LL NEED

* Paper plate, about 11 inches (28 cm) in diameter
* Newspaper or plastic to cover your working area
* Ruler or measuring tape
* Lid or other round object about 5–6 inches (15–18 cm) in diameter, or a compass
* Pencil, pen, or marker
* Scissors
* Paint brush
* Gold acrylic paint
* Elmer's glue (or Gem-Tac permanent glue for a stronger hold)
* Small green sequins

1. Place a large paper plate on newspaper or plastic. Keep the bottom side of the plate facing up.

2. Place the lid at the center of the plate, then slide it away from yourself until it is about 1 inch (2.5 cm) from the far edge of the plate (or use a compass to draw a circle the same size at the same spot).

3. If you are using a lid, use the pencil or pen to trace around its edge, then remove the lid.

4. Draw a line from the far end of the circle you drew to the edge of the plate just past it.

5. Use scissors to cut along the line, then around the outline of the circle.

6. Try on the collar. If the opening is too small, use the scissors to widen the circle.

7. Place the plate facedown on your working surface.

8. Use a paintbrush and undiluted gold acrylic paint to color the plate. Leave it about 20–30 minutes. Gently dab it with a paper towel to check if it's dry—if not, wait 10 or so minutes and check it again.

9. Use the glue to mark small dots on the plate, where you want the gems to be placed.

10. Place a sequin on each dot. Leave it at least 10 minutes to dry (touch the sequins gently to see if the glue is dry before you pick up the collar).

11. Wear proudly.

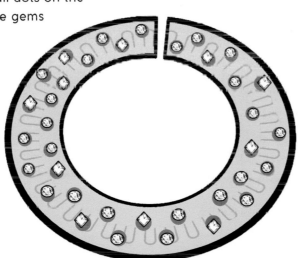

C. S. Lewis. *Topfoto*

members called themselves Kolbitar (Icelandic for "coal biters") because they sat so close to the fire that they could almost taste the coal. After joining the club, Lewis discovered that the myths of northern Europe thrilled him as much as they thrilled Tolkien.

Lewis and Tolkien still disagreed about the nature of myths. Lewis thought that, because myths did not describe real events, they were ultimately lies. Tolkien thought that myths could be a powerful source of truth, showing that people

71

from many nations, from ancient times, had a sense of realities that are beyond this world.

Lewis started to change his mind on the night of September 20, 1931, during an after-dinner walk and conversation with Tolkien and another friend, Hugo Dyson, on Addison's Walk, a pleasant, tree-lined footpath around a small island in the River Cherwell. The conversation continued in Lewis's room. Tolkien left at three o'clock in the morning, while Lewis and Dyson kept talking for another hour.

Part of the conversation had to do with Christianity, which Lewis, for some time, had considered to be a myth and therefore a lie. Tolkien asked Lewis to consider whether some myths that Lewis found so moving, about gods that sacrificed themselves for humans and then came back to life, could point to an event that actually happened in history. Lewis had never thought about it this way.

Later, Lewis said this conversation helped him to return to his Christian faith. This became evident in his writings, which had a clear Christian message. Tolkien, however, despite being deeply religious, preferred to keep his beliefs understated, letting the story itself move his readers.

THE INKLINGS

Tolkien and Lewis joined a group of Oxford writers known as the Inklings. The group was created by a student as a way for writers to read their work to others and get feedback. The student hatched the idea for the group from a play on words: *inkling* means "hint" or "intuition," but it also contains the word *ink*, the essential material used by writers.

The Inklings had much in common. They believed in the power of words and disliked industrialization. They enjoyed discussing history and languages, religion and philosophy, and myths and legends—particularly those from the forgotten Middle Ages. They liked to live simple lives full of ordinary things and wore simple clothes in a college where many strove for elegance and refinement.

Many of the Inklings had fought in the war, and all had been touched by it. Later on, in the confusing and depressing years just before and

Addison's Walk, near Magdalen College. *Jon West, Creative Commons license*

during World War II, they retold stories of long-gone heroes, courage, loyalty, friendship, enchantment, and hope, and they found fresh ways to communicate them to a new generation.

Lewis's room at Magdalen College became the main meeting place for their literary meetings on Thursday evenings. Sometimes they met in a pub—most frequently at the Eagle and Child on St. Giles'—but that was for chatting about the latest news rather than reading their work. The Inklings, and Lewis in particular, were a great encouragement to Tolkien and did much to help him complete *The Hobbit*.

By the time Tolkien finished a first draft of *The Hobbit*, Lewis had come to deeply admire his friend's writing skills. He was particularly impressed by *Lay of Leithian*, a long poem that told in verse the story of Beren and Lúthien, which Ronald had first imagined years ago on his walk in the woods with Edith. Lewis was also fascinated by *The Hobbit* and encouraged Tolkien to continue working on it.

SOLVING PROBLEMS AT HOME

From time to time, Lewis visited the Tolkiens' home, delighting the children with new books. Edith was not too happy about his visits, though. She had not been adjusting well to life in Oxford. Back in Leeds, in spite of all the challenges, she had had a group of friends; here in Oxford, she was mostly alone. She didn't feel at home around other Oxford wives, nor in the academic conversations that were common in most social gatherings.

The Eagle and the Child.
Adam.thomp07, Creative Commons license

She still enjoyed playing the piano but had nowhere but her living room to put her talents to use. She also began to feel resentful of the religion she had adopted for her husband's sake.

All this created a rift that only deepened when her husband became particularly strict in his religious practices, often going to Mass early in the morning on weekdays. And her frequent headaches didn't help the situation.

The time Ronald spent with the Inklings—especially Lewis—was just one more frustration. Ronald seemed to be a different person when he was with the Inklings, sharing things he didn't

73

confide in Edith. Besides, because of Ronald's loud snoring and his habit of keeping late hours, he and Edith slept in different rooms, so their time together had become even more limited. Sometimes, her frustrations grew into anger.

Ronald loved Edith dearly. When he understood her pain, he tried to stay home as much as he could, even if this meant skipping some of the Inklings' meetings. He also recognized her religious doubts and didn't insist that she attend church.

Apart from these problems, they still had a lot in common. They were both devoted parents, they loved art and beauty, and Edith was still always an enthusiastic supporter of his writings.

THE HOBBIT GOES TO PRINT

Tolkien typed the final copy of his full-length novel, by then titled *The Hobbit: Or, There and Back Again*, and in 1936 sent it along with a map to the publisher George Allen & Unwin. The head of the company, Stanley Unwin, read it and gave it to his ten-year-old son Rayner to get his opinion.

Rayner's report included a short summary of the book and his opinion of it: "This book, with the help of maps, does not need any illustrations. It is good and should appeal to all children between the ages of 5 and 9."

Unwin decided to publish the book and sent Tolkien a contract. From then on, an editor worked with Tolkien to make sure both author and publisher were satisfied with the end result. The process took a long time.

The Hobbit was finally published on September 21, 1937, complete with illustrations. Even though Rayner didn't think they were necessary, Stanley thought they would be an important addition and asked Tolkien to provide them. Tolkien obliged, even though he thought a professional artist would do a better job.

The Hobbit was an immediate success, so much so that the publisher had to produce a second printing in December. Tolkien was surprised but happy.

Lots of fan letters arrived in Tolkien's mailbox, while reviews filled the papers. One of the first

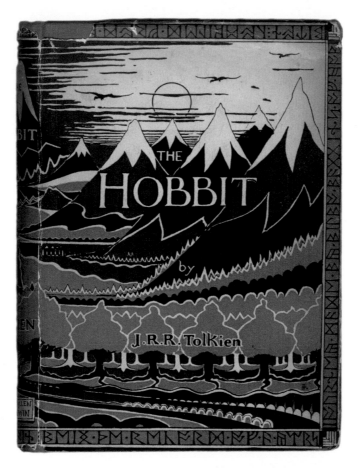

The first edition of *The Hobbit*. This image, featured on the dust jacket of the book, was produced by Tolkien. Initially, Tolkien wanted to paint the dust jacket in four colors: green, blue, black, and red, but each color created an additional expense for the publisher, who eventually asked Tolkien to skip red.

Topfoto

reviewers was C. S. Lewis, who noticed in *The Hobbit* a combination of humor, scholarly study, poetry, and understanding of children the likes of which he had never seen before.

One reason for the book's success was that Tolkien had created (or subcreated, as he would say) not just a story with interesting characters but a whole world to explore. Most readers also admired it as a great piece of literature and felt inspired by the many lessons about courage, friendship, the conflict between good and evil, appreciation for the small things in life, and much more.

Furthermore, many found it easier to identify with Bilbo—the simple hobbit who learns to rise to a challenge but can happily return to his hole in the ground when all is done—than with powerful heroes who are always brave and true.

THE SEARCH FOR A SEQUEL

The Hobbit was so successful that Stanley Unwin began to ask Tolkien for a sequel. Tolkien thought he didn't have much more to say about Hobbits. But he had lots to say about the world where they lived. That world was described in detail in *The Silmarillion,* a project that had grown out of *The Book of Lost Tales.* Over one lunch with Unwin in London, Tolkien proposed the publication of *The Silmarillion,* or else one of the many children's tales Tolkien had already written, such as *Roverandom, Farmer Giles,* and *Mr. Bliss.*

Rayner read *Roverandom* and *Farmer Giles* and gave a positive report, but his father didn't think they could be published as single volumes. *The*

Write a Short Book Review

The Hobbit was not the only book Rayner reviewed. His father believed that books written for children should be reviewed by children. He paid Rayner one shilling for a written report (the equivalent of about $3 today). Rayner's role was important. Without his positive review, The Hobbit might not have been published by George Allen & Unwin. Pretend you have been asked to judge whether a book is fit for publication.

YOU'LL NEED

❋ A book you have read or want to read

❋ Pen or pencil (or computer and printer)

1. Choose a book you have recently read.

2. Write a short paragraph to summarize the book's contents.

3. Now pretend that the book has not been published and that it has been submitted to you. Write your opinion about the story. Is it well written? Will it catch the interest of other readers? If so, what is the recommended age? If it were to be published today, do you think it needs maps or illustrations?

4. (Optional) Post your review on Amazon or Goodreads for other readers to read.

Did you know that some publishers send free books to reviewers? If you like reading and enjoyed writing this review, you may want to contact a few publishers and offer your services. Then watch your library grow!

Draw a Map for a Story

Tolkien found that maps of areas and buildings were important in helping him to track the movements of his characters, just as drawings helped him to visualize their surroundings. He also believed they would be useful to his readers. Do you agree? See for yourself.

YOU'LL NEED

❋ Paper

❋ Pencil and eraser

❋ Computer and printer (optional)

1. Choose a story you have read or written

2. Use pencil and paper to draw a map for the story. If the story doesn't specify where the places are situated, you can decide their location. It can be the map of an area or a building. For example, you could make a map of the route Little Red Riding Hood took to go to her grandmother's house or a map of the house of the three bears that Goldilocks visited. Be as detailed as possible, and take your time. Tolkien changed his first map of *The Lord of the Rings* so many times that he had to glue new paper on top of the old map in places to start anew. He also had to tape pieces of paper to the sides when he realized he needed more room.

3. Once you are satisfied with the map, try to rewrite the story adding details about the characters' movements through the area you have drawn.

4. Compare the new version of the story with the one you had before. Do the new details make it more interesting? Do they make the story easier to describe?

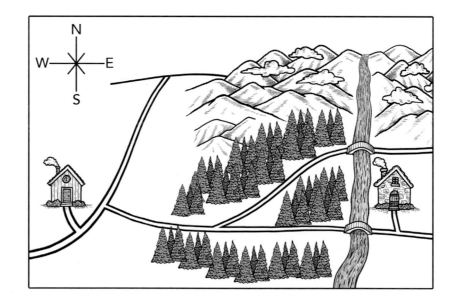

Silmarillion was another story. Unwin gave one of its chapters to adult reviewers, but the result was not encouraging. One reviewer thought it was "of a very thin, if not always downright bad, quality." Unwin didn't tell Tolkien about this review.

It's a good thing that he didn't, because Tolkien had always had mixed feelings about *The Silmarillion.* He had spent much time on it, describing in detail the world he was imagining and creating a set of languages for it. Part of him felt it was important, while another part of him wondered if it was just nonsense. That's why he always hesitated to share it with others, even if the first public reading of one of its tales had been met with applause.

In any case, Unwin listened to the reviewers and kept pressing Tolkien to write something new, something similar to *The Hobbit*. That was easier said than done. Bilbo's journey was over, and so was his progress (what writers would call "character arc") from hesitant to heroic. Tolkien had invested so much in *The Hobbit* that it was difficult to find anything else to say. In order to write a sequel, he needed to find an element in *The Hobbit* that could link in a new story. But what? He explored different possibilities and wrote several versions of the first chapter.

The work proceeded slowly, with many rewritings and corrections. Several times, Tolkien wondered if this sequel would ever come to fruition. Ten years later, when the manuscript was still unfinished, Lewis said that Tolkien worked "like a coral insect"—slowly and out of sight, but with amazing end results. In reality, a study of his works shows that Tolkien had sudden bursts of energy and creativity—only the revision work was done slowly and steadily.

Runes

The writing around the edge of *The Hobbit*'s dust jacket is in runes, an alphabet once used by Scandinavians and Anglo-Saxons. It was typically scratched or carved into wood or stone. In *The Hobbit*, Tolkien used the Anglo-Saxon version (also known as *futhorc* or *fuþorc*) with a few modifications and additional characters. When his readers showed interest in learning this type of writing, Tolkien suggested to the publisher that they should add a runic alphabet to *The Hobbit*.

Later, Tolkien created new, related runic alphabets for other populations of Middle-earth.

A version of Anglo-Saxon futhorc, the type of runes Tolkien used in The Hobbit, with a few modifications.
Wikimedia, Archives of Pearson Scott Foresman

Make Mushroom Toast

Hobbits love to eat. When they are able, they eat as many as six or seven meals per day. And in trying times, food serves as a source of comfort for them. Throughout his journey, Bilbo keeps dreaming of going back home to his comfortable hole where he could live in peace and eat to his heart's content.

Bacon and eggs are some of their favorite foods. When Bilbo is abandoned in a dark tunnel in Goblin-town, he imagines himself in his kitchen frying those two treats. Since Hobbits are also—like Tolkien—fond of mushrooms, this recipe combines all three of these ingredients. Try it out and keep it in mind if a hobbit ever comes knocking on your door.

ADULT SUPERVISION REQUIRED

YOU'LL NEED

- ❋ Cutting board
- ❋ Kitchen knife
- ❋ 1 clove of garlic
- ❋ 1 sprig of parsley
- ❋ Mixing bowl
- ❋ 4 or 5 white or cremini mushrooms (or ¼ lb. of any mushrooms in your local grocery store)
- ❋ Paper towels
- ❋ 1 tablespoon cooking oil
- ❋ Frying pan
- ❋ Mixing spoon
- ❋ Water
- ❋ 1 slice of bacon
- ❋ 1 egg
- ❋ 1 slice of bread
- ❋ Toaster
- ❋ Salt

1. With an adult's help, use the knife to chop the garlic and parsley on a cutting board then set them aside, keeping the two ingredients separate.

2. Place the mushrooms in the bowl, then wash them in the sink under running water.

3. Dry them with the paper towel, then slice them on the cutting board.

4. Add a tablespoon of oil to a frying pan over high heat and fry the mushrooms until nicely browned.

5. Lower the heat to medium, then add the garlic to the pan and cook while stirring for a minute or so, until the garlic is golden.

6. Add the parsley to the pan and cook while stirring for a few seconds.

7. Add one tablespoon of water. Bring the water to a boil, then cover the pan, turn the heat to low, and let it simmer for one minute. Then remove the lid, scoop out the mushroom mixture, and set it aside.

8. Cover a plate with two paper towels.

9. Clean and dry the frying pan, then cook the bacon over medium-low heat,

flipping once or twice as needed, until both sides are crispy.

10. Take the bacon out of the pan and lay it on the paper towel–covered plate.

11. Keep the bacon grease in the pan and use it to fry the egg "sunny-side-up" over low heat. If you want to make sure the egg white is well cooked, drop a table-spoon of water into the pan and cover it quickly with a lid for a minute or so. Turn off the stove and remove the egg from the pan.

12. Toast a slice of bread in a toaster.

13. Place the toasted bread on a plate and top it first with the bacon, then with the egg, and finally with the mushrooms. Sprinkle a little salt over the top.

14. Serve and enjoy!

This recipe is for one person. If you enjoyed it, try repeating it in a larger quantity for your family and friends.

The Leaf and the Tree

From 1938 through 1939, while Tolkien tried to write a sequel for *The Hobbit,* he wrote a short story called "Leaf by Niggle."

It's the tale of a painter who decides to paint a leaf that flies into his room. Soon, he finds he cannot stop there and starts painting more until he finds himself painting a whole tree. But it's a tree he never seems to finish, because all the duties of daily life prevent him from doing so, especially a pesky neighbor who doesn't under-stand what the point is.

Tolkien was, in some ways, in the same situation, with a full-time job, his obligations to write scholarly papers, his duties at home, the needs of his growing children, the many letters he was receiving from fans. . . .

7

THE LORD OF THE RINGS

WORLD WAR II BROKE out in 1939, at a time when both Ronald and Edith were suffering from poor health. In fact, Edith's complaints were so serious that the doctors did some tests to make sure she did not have cancer. They finally ruled it out, but the ordeal must have caused the family serious concern. And just a month before the war, Ronald had an accident that required stitches and resulted in a concussion.

Frodo, Sam, and Gollum walking through the Dead Marshes.
Ted Nasmith

In spite of all this, Tolkien wanted to do what he could for his country. He joined the fire-watching squad and enlisted as a reserve air-raid warden. His tasks included checking that the citizens in his area limited their use of lights in order to prevent the enemy's planes from seeing the buildings. He also had to be ready to sound the alarm when needed. These duties required him to stay up late at night or sleep in one of the huts provided for these servicemen—both challenging arrangements for a middle-aged man.

At home, his vegetable garden became especially important when food rations were restricted. And Edith's aviary—as lovely as it was—had to be turned into a more practical coop where the family could raise chickens for eggs and meat.

The war created a new set of concerns for Tolkien's sons. In November 1939, 22-year-old John went to Rome, Italy, to prepare to become a Catholic priest. But Italy's alliance with Nazi Germany made Rome a dangerous place for British citizens.

In May 1940, John and a few other seminarians fled Italy dressed as civilians (rather than priests) and managed to take the last boat available to cross the channel from France to England before the German troops occupied France.

John continued to study as a seminarian, working at the same time as a head gardener in order to make ends meet during the difficult wartime. This way, he combined two passions he had learned from his father: a commitment to the Roman Catholic Church and a love for plants. He was ordained a priest in February 1946.

Michael, not yet 19 at the start of the war, volunteered for army service, but was required to spend one year at university. He spent it in Oxford, studying history, then he was enrolled as an anti-aircraft gunman, mostly defending English airfields. Injured during training, he was admitted to an army hospital where he met a lovely nurse, Joan Griffiths, and fell in love.

By the next year, they were ready to marry. Ronald sent Michael a couple of letters, recommending a longer engagement, but the couple chose to marry anyhow, in a quiet ceremony.

Michael continued to serve in the war until 1943, when he was dismissed because of a serious injury. Ronald lamented how difficult it was for Michael to find a good job, even though he had earned a good degree and the prestigious George Medal, for acts of great bravery.

Christopher was the last of the Tolkien boys to enlist. He joined the Royal Air Force in July 1943, at age 18. The next year, he was sent to South Africa to train as a Spitfire pilot and stayed there until 1945, when the war ended. Ronald kept in close communication with him by mail. Of all his children, Christopher was the one Ronald found most similar to himself.

Christopher had always shown great writing and editing skills, so Tolkien mailed him every chapter of the new book he was trying to write, one by one, and asked for his opinion. Christopher's comments were important to Tolkien, both as encouragement and detailed advice.

At the same time, Ronald shared his son some fatherly guidance, drawn from his own

Grow a Little Garden

Gardening was an important activity for Ronald. Besides passing on this skill to John, he mentioned it often in his books. Sam Gamgee, one of the main characters of The Lord of the Rings, *was a gardener, and many of the inhabitants of Middle-earth loved plants.*

You can experience some of the joys of gardening by growing a few small plants in your home. Many herbs and vegetables are easy to grow. Since green beans are one of the easiest plants to grow, you will use them in this activity. Wait for early or late spring (depending on the climate), because they need some warmth and sunshine.

YOU'LL NEED

- ❋ Bowl
- ❋ Water
- ❋ 8 green-bean seeds (you can buy a package online or from a plant nursery)
- ❋ 2 leftover plastic containers of strawberries, kiwis, or grapes (with holes on the bottom)
- ❋ Soil
- ❋ Tray (or other rimmed surface to place the containers on)
- ❋ Planter vase

1. Soak the seeds in water overnight.

2. Fill the containers with soil and place them on a tray or another rimmed surface where excessive water can drain without damaging anything or making a mess.

3. Use your finger to poke holes in the soil, one near each of the corners of the containers. The holes should be about 1 inch (2.5 cm) deep.

4. Place one of the soaked beans into each hole.

5. Keep the soil moist but not soggy by watering lightly each day. Too much water can cause the seeds to crack and stop them from germinating. If the containers have tops, you can close them to create a greenhouse effect that helps the plants grow.

6. After 7 to 10 days, you should see some sprouts. If you closed the containers' lids, open them once you see sprouts poking through the soil. Note that some of the beans will probably not sprout.

7. After a few more days, the sprouts will grow some leaves.

8. When the plants begin to grow tall enough, you may remove them to a bigger planter, keeping some space between them.

9. It will take two to three months from the time you first plant the seeds to see the first green beans.

If you don't like green beans, you can try this activity with other seeds. In that case, follow the instructions on the package of the seeds you choose.

experience. Even if Christopher never experienced the horror of the trenches, flying fighter planes was a dangerous occupation. Ronald encouraged him by reminding him that there is more to life than what we see in our limited experience: "Keep up your hobbitry in heart, and think that all *stories* feel like that when you are *in* them. You are inside a very great story!"

War was naturally a constant subject in this correspondence between father and son, and Ronald made frequent connections with the portion of new story Christopher was helping him to write at that time: one of the most crucial parts of the hobbits' journey. This portion included many references to war, such as the hobbits' walk through the Dead Marshes: a network of muddy pits filled with dead faces that, as Tolkien admitted in a later letter, "owe something to Northern France after the Battle of the Somme."

But Ronald reminded Christopher that things in life are not "as clear cut as in a story." People are not always neatly divided into good and bad people. "We have started out with a great many Orcs on our side," he wrote.

When Christopher returned from the war in 1945, he was made a permanent member of the Inklings. He was put in charge of reading out loud the manuscript of *The Lord of the Rings* to the other members, because they thought he read it better than his father. He soon resumed his studies at Oxford's Trinity College, in subjects that were very similar to the ones his father had taken.

THE NEW STORY TAKES SHAPE

With Christopher's help and the encouragement of the other Inklings, Tolkien continued to write his new book, even while enemy airplanes flew over his head. Priscilla, the only child still at home, helped him by typing, with just two fingers, the first chapters. He had finally found a link to connect *The Hobbit* to his new story: the Ring that Bilbo had taken from Gollum.

In *The Hobbit*, the Ring doesn't seem very powerful, but what if it was? Tolkien built his new story around this possibility. The story starts about sixty years after the events of *The Hobbit*, with Bilbo back at home in his hobbit-hole with many lessons learned and Gollum's Ring still in his pocket.

Two Mustangs and a Spitfire, two types of aircrafts used during World War II. *Jez, Creative Commons license*

At the start of the book, Bilbo gets ready for his "eleventy-first birthday," as he called it. He is turning 111, a very special age. What's more, his favorite cousin, Frodo Baggins, is turning 33 on the same day, September 22. And 33 is when Hobbits officially come of age. This occasion calls for special gifts. That's when Bilbo decides to give Frodo his will and papers confirming him as his heir.

But the wizard Gandalf encourages Bilbo to do more: that is, to give Frodo the Ring. This takes more than gentle persuasion. In the end, Bilbo agrees, gives Frodo the Ring, and leaves the Shire—the land of the Hobbits. Gandalf tells Frodo to be careful with the Ring and to keep it secret.

Seventeen years later, Gandalf comes back with more warnings. The Ring is a creation of Sauron, the evil servant of the Dark Lord Melkor, who aims at the destruction of Middle-earth.

As such, the Ring has the potential to control and enslave others and bring great evil to the world. Sauron has been trying to get it back, and the Ring, possessing some sort of life of its own, is attempting to return to its owner. Sauron has learned that the Ring is in the Shire and will certainly soon attack.

There is only one remedy: the Ring has to be cast into the Cracks of Doom, at the heart of Sauron's country, where it was originally forged. Only then will the Ring be destroyed forever. Gandalf warns Frodo not to try to use the Ring against Sauron, because anyone who uses the Ring's power will simply become another Dark Lord.

Like Bilbo in *The Hobbit*, Frodo has no desire to leave his comfortable home in the Shire. But he understands that the situation is too dreadful to be ignored. Someone has to save his land. Whether he likes it or not, he understands that the task falls on his shoulders.

Obeying the call, Frodo takes with him his faithful friend and gardener Samwise Gamgee and a cousin named Peregrin Took, best known as "Pippin." Another cousin, Meriadoc "Merry" Brandybuck, joins them later. Along the way, the hobbits meet the warrior Aragorn, who is sent by Gandalf to lead them.

Gandalf, as depicted in the 2001 movie *The Lord of the Rings: The Fellowship of the Ring*, directed by Peter Jackson
Photofest

(right) **Frodo and Sam as they are pictured in Peter Jackson's 2003 movie,** *The Lord of the Rings: The Two Towers.* **It shows the moment when the two hobbits see the Black Gates of Mordor and Gollum tells them there is another way to enter.** *Photofest*

(below) **The Black Riders, as pictured in the 2001 movie** *The Lord of the Rings: The Fellowship of the Ring,* **directed by Peter Jackson.** *Photofest*

The rest of the story is one adventure after another, with Sauron's Ringwraiths, dressed as Black Riders, attacking the group and inflicting a serious wound on Frodo. Eventually, though, the hobbits make it to Rivendell, where they meet Gandalf and three more warriors: the valiant Boromir, the Elven prince Legolas, and the dwarf Gimli. These, together with Gandalf, Aragorn, and the hobbits, form the Fellowship of the Ring, united in the same heroic mission to take the Ring to Mordor and destroy it.

After a while, the group divides, and two stories continue at the same time. While Frodo and Sam keep on their journey, the others fight in the War of the Ring between Sauron and the Free Peoples of the World (all those not under Sauron's domination).

Gollum is back in the story, this time as a questionable, annoying guide for Frodo and Sam.

Along the way, he tests Sam's patience and raises high suspicions in Faramir, Boromir's brother, who encourages Frodo to part ways with Gollum. But Frodo feels sorry for Gollum and treats him with kindness. In the end, in an unexpected twist of events, Gollum ends up saving Frodo from falling to the power of the Ring and brings the Ring to destruction.

Finally, Aragorn, the rightful king of Arnor and Gondor, is restored to the throne and crowned king of the Reunited Kingdom. Frodo, Sam, Merry, and Pippin return to the Shire to find that it has fallen under the control of the Wizard Saruman. Saruman's men have ruined the Shire by cutting down trees and replacing the old mill with a new, mechanized one that polluted the land. In the end, one of Saruman's servants kills him, ending the wizard's rule.

Sam, Pippin, and Merry prepare to settle back into the saved Shire and readjust to their previous lifestyle, but Frodo can't. Ultimately, he is allowed to cross the sea with Bilbo, Gandalf, and the elves Elrond and Galadriel. The book ends with Sam, who left the Shire as a helper to Frodo but has often behaved like a leader. In the last scene, his wife Rose welcomes him home, pulls up a chair for him at the table, and puts his little daughter, Elanor, on his lap. "He drew a deep breath. 'Well, I'm back,' he said."

PUBLISHING PAINS

Tolkien wrote the story as if he were experiencing it together with his characters, discovering each new situation with them. For example, when Frodo and Sam left the Shire, Tolkien was as unsure as they were of what would happen next. When the group met the first Black Rider, Tolkien initially thought it was Gandalf.

Some characters just "appeared" in his story. One of these was Faramir, "I am sure I did not invent him," Tolkien wrote. "I did not even want him, though I like him, but there he came walking into the woods of Ithilien."

As he kept writing, he realized this book was quite different from *The Hobbit*. The plot was certainly more serious and complicated. Priscilla's

The Shadow of Sauron, as portrayed by the artist Ted Nasmith. *Ted Nasmith*

Trees in Tolkien's Stories

Tolkien expressed his love for trees in his stories by giving them important roles. The older Elves even taught trees to speak, so they could communicate with them. And trees provided refuge in times of danger. In *The Hobbit,* the dwarves climbed on a larch, a fir, and pine trees to escape a pack of wolves (and propped Bilbo up, who could not climb).

In our world, plants are often mistreated and have no way of defending themselves, but in Middle-earth they are respected and valued, with a race of creatures—the Ents—who are assigned specifically to their protection. The Ents looked like giant trees but could walk and talk. Their language was beautiful but long-winded, because the Ents wouldn't say anything that was not worth an investment of time for both speaker and hearer.

The oldest of the Ents was Treebeard, who taught Merry and Pippin a lesson about taking their time rather than act in haste.

The Ents played a crucial part in the War of the Ring. When the corrupted wizard Saruman began to cut down Fangorn Forest in order to fuel the machineries he had built inside the fortress of Isengard, the Ents went on the attack. The forest was huge. To reach the other side, Treebeard carried Merry and Pippin 70,000 Ent-strides, or about 100 miles (160 km). In the end, they expelled Saruman and his forces, destroyed his machines, and filled Isengard with orchards and trees.

This might be what Tolkien wished people would do with much of the machinery that had been built—and continued to be built—as a result of the Industrial Revolution. He greatly disliked this aspect of human "progress" and considered it dangerous.

The most beautiful trees in *The Lord of the Rings* were the silvery mallorn trees, which grow only in the forest of Lothlórien. Mallorns don't lose their leaves during the winter. Their leaves turn gold in the fall, but stay on the trees until spring, when they are replaced by green leaves, while golden flowers begin to bloom.

When Sam left Lothlòrien, the mighty elf Galadriel gave him a box of soil infused with her magical powers and containing one single mallorn nut, which Sam could later grow into a tree.

Not all trees are good in Middle-earth. Old Man Willow, for example, hates all walking creatures. In *The Lord of the Rings*, he trapped Merry and Pippin inside his trunk and tipped Frodo into a stream. Only the mysterious Tom Bombadil was able to calm the tree.

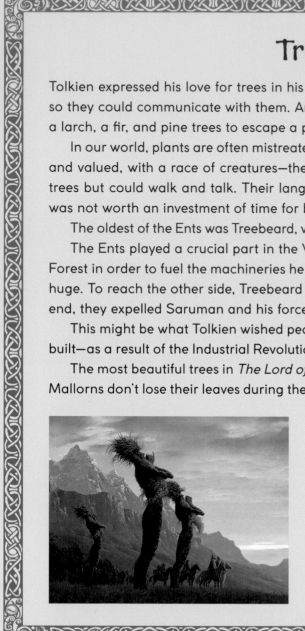

The Ents, as imagined by the artist Ted Nasmith. *Ted Nasmith*

fright when she typed about the Black Riders made him wonder if the story was too scary for young readers. Would Unwin be happy with the end result?

Also, the new book included many of the characters and places that Tolkien had described in *The Silmarillion*, so Tolkien was more convinced than ever that *The Silmarillion* should be published before or together with the new story.

In 1949, he was introduced to Milton Waldman, a senior editor for the publishing house William Collins. Waldman was interested in *The Lord of the Rings* and *The Silmarillion* and said he would consider publishing both.

Tolkien was pleased but still felt bound to Unwin, who had originally asked for a sequel. But he warned Unwin that *The Lord of the Rings* was not a children's book, nor was it a sequel to *The Hobbit*. Rather, it was a sequel to *The Silmarillion*, and should be published together with it. By the way, he said, both books together would amount to more than a million words.

Unwin was willing to make compromises, such as publishing the two works as three or four separate volumes, or taking portions of *The Silmarillion* and adding them to *The Lord of the Rings*. But Tolkien, confident in Waldman's offer, pressed Unwin to give an immediate and definite answer: was he willing to publish both works or not? Under pressure, Unwin said no—he later indicated that he might have said yes if Tolkien had given him more time.

Free from his obligation to Unwin, Tolkien contacted Waldman again. Initially, all seemed

Faringdon Folly Tower, near Oxford, was built in 1935 among much controversy, since many of the locals disapproved the project. According to John Garth, one of the main Tolkien scholars, the controversy might have attracted Tolkien's attention, and Folly tower—seen as a negative symbol—might have inspired some of the towers Tolkien described in his books, such as Saruman's dark tower, known as Orthanc. *Charlie, Flickr*

well, and William Collins invited Tolkien to London to discuss the publication. But the excitement didn't last long. After further consideration, the company asked Tolkien to cut down the number of words in *The Lord of the Rings*. In the meantime, Waldman left the country and passed Tolkien's proposal to some less enthusiastic colleagues who didn't seem interested in moving the projects forward.

Join the Chorus of Middle-Earth

Music is very important in Tolkien's worlds, from the creative songs of Ilúvatar and the disruption of Melkor's song in The Book of Lost Tales *to the Elvish songs in* The Lord of the Rings. *These songs can be powerful (such as the song of Luthién that releases the bonds of winter), playful (such as the song of the dwarves who threaten to break Bilbo's plates), or heroic. They include laments, songs of praise, walking songs, eating songs, and even a bath song, sung by Pippin when he, Frodo, and Sam were able to wash up after a long walk from Hobbiton, the Hobbits' village in the center of the Shire.*

YOU'LL NEED

- ✳ Internet access
- ✳ Paper
- ✳ Pencil or pen

Listen to Tolkien recite the bath song here: https://www.youtube.com/watch?v=Ah6lc45Qi2A.

Then write your own song about some activity you do every day or one you particularly enjoy, such as swimming, playing a sport, playing with friends, or eating your favorite food.

As time passed, Tolkien wondered if either *The Lord of the Rings* or *The Silmarillion* would ever see the light of day. In March 1952, he asked Waldman for a clear answer: Would they publish these books immediately? Once again, he received a negative answer.

At the same time, both Stanley and Rayner Unwin wrote Tolkien encouraging letters, letting him know that their door was still open. Tolkien answered that he had changed his mind and was willing to see at least a portion of his work published.

FINISHING THE BOOK AND VISITING GONDOR

Ronald worked hard to get *The Lord of the Rings* ready for Unwin. By that time, he lived near a busy intersection and found the noise to be distracting. He did some editing at his son Michael's house in Woodcote, a village in south Oxfordshire. On March 30, 1953, he and Edith found a quieter residence at 76 Sandfield Road, Oxford, but even there, the peace didn't last long. The road, initially a cul-de-sac, became open to through-traffic, letting in a stream of cars and scooters.

That, Tolkien said, was in addition to the usual noise their neighbors made with radios, televisions, and dogs. Ten years later, Tolkien added to his list of complaints a group of young men who started to practice some Beatles-style music near his home.

In spite of all this, Tolkien finished the manuscript, and Rayner Unwin and his wife traveled to

Oxford to pick it up. Rayner was impressed, and wrote a letter to his father (who was at that time in the Far East) to recommend publication. Rayner was honest about the risks. Publishing such a large work might cost as much as 1,000 British pounds (the equivalent of about 35,000 pounds or 40,000 dollars today). But Rayner believed it was worth it.

Stanley trusted his son's judgment but told Tolkien that their company would not pay him royalties until their up-front costs were recovered. Tolkien agreed.

Before publication, Tolkien had to make another compromise: dividing the work into separate books. Tolkien suggested six (since he had divided the story into six parts), but Unwin wanted three. In the end, Tolkien complied, and *The Lord of the Rings* appeared in three volumes as *The Fellowship of the Ring*, *The Two Towers*, and *The Return of the King*, published between July 1954 and October 1955. Tolkien had suggested other titles, but in the end, he again gave in to the publisher's choices.

In the summer of 1955, while he was still writing the appendixes to *The Lord of the Rings*, Ronald took a vacation with his daughter Priscilla while Edith went on a Mediterranean cruise with friends. Ronald and Priscilla's destination was Italy, particularly the cities of Venice and Assisi. As he prepared for his trip, he told a friend he was off to Gondor (the South Kingdom of the Númenóreans in Middle-earth) to tour its harbor, Pelargir (which he envisioned to be Venice), and the flowery valleys of Lossarnach (which he imagined to be Assisi). Gondor was certainly on

his mind during his travels, because it plays an important part in *The Return of the King*—the book Ronald had edited last.

He found Venice more beautiful than he had expected and quite different from anything he had ever seen. The cloudy weather enhanced the gray-scale colors of the city, making it appear "elvishly lovely." Besides its beauty, Venice offered another benefit for Tolkien: there were no cars. Tolkien was also surprised to discover that the Italian language was not as emphatic and exaggerated as he had thought, and he regretted that he had not learned more of it before this trip.

From Venice, Ronald and Priscilla went to Florence and then Assisi, the small town where St.

A view of Venice at night.
Luca Sartoni, Flickr

Francis, one of the most famous Roman Catholic saints, lived between the 12th and the 13th centuries. Ronald was impressed by the masterful frescos he found in the churches and by the tranquility and simplicity of the place. He found it conducive to prayer and worship—in spite of a sermon that went on so long he had to leave the church through a side door.

Some minor problems during this trip included relentless summer mosquitoes and crowded trains with passengers pushing in every direction to get in and out. Overall, however, Italy left a great impression on Ronald, who would return years later on a cruise with Edith.

MIXED REVIEWS

Initially, the reviews for *The Lord of the Rings* were mixed. Some readers, who expected another book like *The Hobbit*, were puzzled. It was definitely not a children's book, and it was different from the typical heroic stories. Many critics didn't know how to define it. One called it "super science fiction." Others disliked fantasy in general and thought it

A view of Assisi.
Chris Yunker, Flickr

Fantasy, Escape, and Eucatastrophe

Tolkien thought reading and writing fantasy could be very important. For one thing, it can free the mind to see things in a new light. Many discover that after "traveling" to a world of fantasy, they see our world with new eyes—even ordinary, everyday things that most people don't notice anymore.

Some of Tolkien's critics thought that fantasy was useless, just an escape from the "real world." In a later speech, Tolkien explained that escape is not always bad. Escaping from an enemy, for example, can be heroic. Looking away from the evils of this world can sometimes be a good thing for those who, like Tolkien, believe there really is something better.

Deep down, Tolkien said, everyone wishes they could escape the worst things in life. That's why people like happy endings. Tolkien coined a special name for the happy endings common in fairy stories. He called them **eucatastrophes**, adding the Greek prefix *eu* (meaning "good") to the word *catastrophe*.

Like catastrophes, eucatastrophes are sudden and unexpected, upsetting the order of things. But eucatastrophes do it in a positive way, turning things for the better and bringing tears of joyful relief. One example of eucatastrophe is the moment in *The Hobbit* when Bilbo thinks everything is lost and the Great Eagles suddenly appear and come to his rescue.

To Tolkien, eucatastrophes were not just artificial happy endings to make readers happy. He truly believed that, even if our own world seems full of terrible catastrophes and painful sorrow, there is somehow "Joy beyond the walls of the world."

was not a suitable form of writing for a college professor.

Some tried to find hidden meanings. They thought the book was an allegory, especially of World War II, since it was published soon after the war. Tolkien disliked this supposition. In fact, he disliked allegories in general.

It's normal for authors to bring some of their experience into their books. Tolkien admitted that some portions of *The Lord of the Rings* were inspired by his memories of war. For example, Tolkien said that Sam Gamgee was a reflection of the common soldiers he had come to admire during World War I.

It's also normal for readers to make connections with their own experiences. But Tolkien never meant to lead people to make these specific connections. In fact, he thought that searching for allegorical meanings distracted readers from the actual story, which is what he wanted them to enjoy.

In any case, the majority of readers was enthusiastic about *The Lord of the Rings* and took it for what it was. C. S. Lewis was probably one of the first to understand its importance, when he called it "the conquest of new territory."

There were many reasons for the books' popularity. They were well written and exciting, with the power to take readers out of this world and plunge them into another that seemed at the same time magical and real. In a weary postwar Europe, where talks of bravery, patriotism, and sacrifice often roused painful and disheartening memories, Tolkien was able to rekindle those values by placing them in a world where they were still stirring, fresh, and real.

Another reason the books were so loved was that the readers could easily identify with characters like Bilbo, Frodo, Sam, Pippin, and Merry—the type of common, unsung heroes who had fought in the two World Wars, often battling their own fears. Tolkien's heroes are often uncertain and weak and fall prey to many temptations, but they manage to keep going.

Even Aragorn, who might look like the typical hero—who has to prove himself worthy through a series of tests and secure his rightful claim to the throne—is often wavering and eventually fails. But it's only once he accepts this failure that he is prepared for victory.

The Ring was so powerful that even Frodo fell prey to its attraction. One of his temptations is pictured here in a scene from the 2001 movie *The Lord of the Rings: The Fellowship of the Ring*, directed by Peter Jackson. Frodo became so afraid and suspicious of those around him that was tempted to use the Ring to become invisible. But Gandalf had warned him of the dangers. The Ring could take over the life of its holder. It could give immortality, but only for an existence without true life. Any mortal who used it often to become invisible would, in the end, fade completely and be consumed by dark power.
Photofest

Turn Your Friends into Heroes

When Frodo and Sam sat discouraged, questioning how to reach their destination and how they would ever return home, Sam wondered if they might be living a story like the old legends they loved, and that one day someone might write a tale about them. Frodo thought it was funny, and he took the joke further by suggesting that Sam would be known as "Samwise the Stouthearted"—which sounds like a hero's name.

Turn your friends into heroes by making up names for them. If possible, try using the same initial letter for both the name and the honorary title, as Frodo did with Sam. You could have Kevin the Kingly, Megan the Magnificent, or Oliver the Outstanding. You can also turn common areas or household objects into magical places. For example, an oven can become the Tomb of Sweltering Fire and a sink the Fountain of Cleansing Waters.

Create other names like these, then see if your friends understand your references.

8

RETIREMENT AND LEGACY

THE LORD OF THE RINGS continued to grow in popularity and began to be translated into other languages. If Unwin ever had the slightest doubt about his investment in these books, it was all forgotten.

It was not long before someone tried to dramatize Tolkien's stories. The first of these requests came in 1953 from St. Margaret's School in Edinburgh, where a teacher asked if her students could perform a stage version of *The Hobbit*.

A reconstruction of Hobbiton, created in New Zealand as a set for Peter Jackson's *The Lord of the Rings* movies. Today, it's a tourist attraction. *djr photography, iStock*

Tolkien was willing to allow these efforts, especially if they were limited to schools and small stages, but he disapproved of plays that changed some portions of the story. In any case, he had to work with his publisher, who encouraged him to allow adaptations that would result in greater sales.

Ronald and Edith in front of their house at 76 Sandfield Road, Oxford, in 1961. *Topfoto*

One of these was the 1955 BBC adaptation of *The Lord of the Rings* for a radio series. Tolkien was not very enthusiastic from the start, and he became particularly disappointed when, after a six-episode run of the first book, the BBC jammed the last two books of the trilogy into the next six episodes. Tolkien expressed some of his doubts to the producer, asking why the book had to be dramatized in the first place. Why not quote portions of the book instead? He never received a reply.

Overall, Tolkien thought his books were not well suited for dramatization. He was especially afraid that a play or movie, being necessarily shorter, would turn into a light and silly fairy tale, losing much of what he had put on the written page. And his fears came true all too often.

In 1957, three Americans visited Tolkien: agent Forrest J. Ackerman, movie director Morton Grady Zimmerman, and producer Al Brodax. They had already asked George Allen & Unwin for authorization to turn *The Lord of the Rings* into an animated movie and wanted to win Tolkien's agreement.

Tolkien was impressed by their thorough preparation, which included good illustrations and photos of charming sceneries. The script, however, disappointed him once again. It looked as though Zimmerman had read *The Lord of the Rings* in a hurry and written a quick screenplay with what little he could remember.

Zimmerman had skipped some major scenes, given priority to the battles instead of the main story, confused some names of places, and introduced elements (such as fairy castles) that were never in the books. Tolkien thought this showed a lack of respect for his original work. The negotiations continued for a while until, in the end, Ackerman dropped the project.

More offers came. Even the Beatles wanted to make a film of *The Lord of the Rings*, with John Lennon as Gollum, Paul McCartney as Frodo, George Harrison as Gandalf, and Ringo Starr as Sam, but they couldn't obtain the rights.

In 1969, however, Tolkien agreed to give United Artists Corporation, an American production company, essentially unlimited rights to use his works in motion pictures. The reasons for this unexpected decision are not entirely clear. He had seen some terrible proposals and, in a letter to his secretary, he expressed his hope that United Artists would prevent the production of tasteless works. But his main reason might have been financial, since, by 1969, the Tolkiens' struggling health had forced them to make a move that required more money than he was receiving through his retirement and royalties. This contract would create several problems after his death, depriving both his publisher and the Tolkien Estate of any control over further deals.

RETIREMENT

The move that weighed heavily on the Tolkiens' finances happened in 1968. Since 1958, when a serious operation had forced Edith to spend much time in a nursing home, the Tolkiens had frequently stayed in a hotel in Bournemouth, a resort town about 94 miles south of Oxford. Due to its

Hotel Miramar, Bournemouth.
Alwyn Ladell, on Flickr.com

mild climate, Bournemouth was a favorite place for elderly people or those who had recently been ill. There, Edith's health continued to improve.

Edith felt at home with the other hotel guests, while Ronald missed the large library and the long conversations he had at Oxford. Still, he was glad to see Edith happy, and he appreciated the quiet surroundings. Besides, both Ronald and Edith enjoyed resting from their home chores and letting others wait on them for a change. They often had visitors, including their young grandson Simon, Christopher's son, who spent a vacation with them.

In spite of this, it was obvious that their health was not what it used to be. Once, when Edith fell and broke her arm, Ronald had to give up a writing commitment in order to care for her. Another time, he had a fainting spell, probably due to stress. Because of this, they spent more time than ever in Bournemouth, until they decided to move there for good. Ronald was free to do so, since he had retired from teaching in 1959.

They rented a bungalow in Poole, about five miles west of Bournemouth. For the first time in their lives, they had central heating and a fancy kitchen, which Edith welcomed with the excitement of a new bride. There were two bedrooms and two bathrooms, so they could each have their private quarters. And there were no stairs, so it

Sunset over the harbor at Poole.
Stephen Colebourne, Flickr

was easier and safer for them to move around, especially since Edith suffered from arthritis and rheumatic pains.

Outside, there was a veranda and a large garden where Ronald and Edith could sit to enjoy the fresh air. In spite of their different interests, they still appreciated each other's company and took frequent walks hand in hand.

With the help of a secretary sent by Rayner Unwin, Ronald turned part of the garage into an office and library. This secretary, Joy Hill, became a great support to the Tolkiens. She assisted Ronald both in keeping up with his legal correspondence and in answering the great quantity of fan letters which were becoming too numerous for him to reply in person.

By this time, Tolkien had learned never to give out his private address, because at Oxford some fans had come to his house uninvited. Many tried to call him on the phone. Some who lived across the globe woke him up in the middle of the night because they didn't remember that England was in a different time zone. He was also pestered by reporters, photographers, and companies that wanted to produce items related to his books. Hill was a great help in sorting out the requests.

In fact, the first time Hill visited the Tolkiens, her arms were so full of letters and presents for him that the packers at the office had attached some packages to her arms with twine. When Ronald saw her, he told Edith that the publisher had sent him "a walking Christmas tree."

Among the presents there was a goblet with the inscription that had been carved in the Ring.

Tolkien appreciated the gesture but, since the inscription was in the Black Speech of Mordor, Sauron's realm, he couldn't in good conscience drink from the goblet and used it as an ashtray instead.

Hill did more than secretarial work. Being in her twenties, she had sufficient youthful energy to assist the Tolkiens, who were dealing with declining health and, being away from their family and Oxford friends, a bit of depression and loneliness. They soon considered her a daughter.

By that time, in fact, all of the Tolkiens' children were living on their own. John was a Catholic priest in Stoke-on-Trent, Staffordshire. Michael had been a teacher in different Catholic schools further north. Christopher had followed in his father's footsteps by becoming a teacher and lecturer at Oxford. And Priscilla had become a tutor in charge of the social work training course at High Wycombe College, Buckinghamshire.

LIFE WITHOUT EDITH

Ronald was often distracted from business and writing by bouts of illness and concerns about Edith's failing health. The final blow came in November 1971, when her gallbladder became inflamed, and she had to spend a week in the hospital. For a while she seemed to be recovering, but she suddenly relapsed, and she died on November 29. She was 82 years old.

Edith's death was very difficult for Ronald, who grieved for months, unable to work, in spite of the support he was receiving from family and friends. The idea of living alone was painful, and he thought of returning to Oxford.

Christopher helped to make this possible by writing to the warden of Merton College, who gladly offered Ronald accommodations at the school and the assistance of a couple who could work as his caretakers.

Tolkien returned to Oxford in March and found comfort in the activities he had always loved. He continued to work on *The Silmarillion* and other tales, poems, and essays that kept sprouting into his mind. Some of these works were published around this time, such as *The Adventures of Tom Bombadil* (a collection of poems) and *Tree and Leaf.* This last book combines his story "Leaf by Niggle" with his essay "On Fairy-Stories," both helpful in understanding the world Tolkien depicted in *The Lord of the Rings* and his choices in describing it.

The Silmarillion, however, seemed far from completion. There might have been several different reasons for this delay. The material was huge and hard to organize while keeping it consistent with Tolkien's other works. Sometimes, revisiting early stories to be included in *The Silmarillion* raised new questions about life in Middle-earth, making the work seem endless. Besides, now that *The Lord of the Rings* had become a success, Tolkien felt pressure to maintain the same high standard for *The Silmarillion.*

In the meantime, he continued to visit his children, grandchildren and, by now, great-grandchildren. Tolkien had always been a fun grandfather. When his grandchildren were young, he took them on walks, sharing his love for nature.

The Fellows' Garden by Merton College was one of Ronald's favorite places. His grandson Michael George remembered 81-year-old Ronald chasing 4-year-old Catherine, Michael George's daughter, around the lime trees in these gardens.

aherrero, Flickr

Always playful, he often ran after them, threatening to catch them with the hooked end of his stick.

He loved to spend Christmastime with them and spent much time decorating the tree and setting up the manger scene. He also assisted them in their studies and encouraged their interests. For example, when he discovered that Joanna, the daughter of his son Michael, was interested in plants and animals, he bought her books to help her to learn more. He also wrote a poem for her about "a fat cat on the mat" who still remembered his noble ancestor, the lion. Tolkien continued the same fun with his great-grandchildren, as long as his strength allowed it.

He also continued to visit his brother Hilary who, by this time, was also a widower with grown children. Hilary still lived at his farm at Evesham, with his oldest son Gabriel, Gabriel's family, and a dog that Hilary called Bilbo when it was good and Baggins when it was bad. Hilary was still proud of his plum trees, but by this time, he had lost much of the energy needed for farming and had to hire outside help. He and Ronald spent most of their time together talking or watching cricket or tennis on TV.

In the meantime, Ronald continued to receive letters of appreciation. In 1972, he received two of the greatest honors of his life. On March 28, he traveled to Buckingham Palace, where Queen Elizabeth II awarded him the prestigious medal of Commander of the Order of the British Empire (CBE). Tolkien felt deeply moved. A second honor—maybe even more meaningful to him—was the honorary Doctorate of Letters he received from Oxford University, the institution he had most loved, for his achievements in the field of philology.

But his strength continued to fade, and he often complained of feeling tired. He died in

Ronald and Edith's grave at Wolvercote Cemetery, Oxford. *Rosa Sierra, Flickr*

Bournemouth, on September 2, 1973, of a chest infection associated with a gastric ulcer. He was buried next to Edith at Wolvercote Cemetery. Their gravestone reads: EDITH MARY TOLKIEN, LUTHIEN, 1889–1971. JOHN RONALD REUEL TOLKIEN, BEREN, 1892–1973.

TOLKIEN LIVES ON

Christopher Tolkien worked on the material his father had left behind, beginning with *The Silmarillion,* which Ronald had always wanted to see in print but had left unfinished and disorganized. The work, done with the assistance of Canadian author Guy Gavriel Kay, was accomplished in four years and published in 1977.

The Silmarillion received mixed reviews. Some were amazed at the detailed description of a world that seemed to be without end. In fact, to this day, some of Tolkien's fans think it is his best work. Others were confused and even frustrated by the great number of names and disappointed that it was not a unified story like *The Hobbit* and *The Lord of the Rings.* But it was never meant to be one.

Christopher saw the editing of *The Silmarillion* as a serious responsibility. At one point, he had a dream that his father was in the house, earnestly looking for something, and Christopher realized with horror that it was *The Silmarillion.* "I was terrified by the idea that he might discover what I had done," he said.

In spite of the criticism, *The Silmarillion* became a bestseller among Tolkien's fans, and was translated into sixteen languages. This showed the publishers that readers were eager to buy anything that Tolkien had written. Christopher then edited other works by his father and incorporated them into a twelve-volume series titled The History of Middle-earth.

This series introduces the readers to Tolkien's unknown writings and insights and arranges his works in chronological order, helping the readers to see how he progressed from one work to another, how he changed some names and events, and what decisions his son had to make in editing. Many find that reading The History of Middle-earth and *The Silmarillion* helps them to better understand and enjoy *The Lord of the Rings*.

BACK ON THE RADIO AND ON THE SCREEN

In spite of the limited success of its first series, in 1981 the BBC aired a new dramatization of *The Lord of the Rings*, this time in 26 half-hour episodes. The following year, it aired the story again in 13 one-hour episodes, which were also released on both cassette tape and CD sets. In spite of a few omissions and changes, it kept quite faithful to Tolkien's story line, and the actors gave a good portrayal of the characters as Tolkien had intended them. Of all the adaptations of Tolkien's works, this remains the one most of his fans seem to prefer.

Turning Tolkien's works into movies, though, seemed like an impossible dream. The first attempt to translate any of Tolkien's writings to the big screen was a 12-minute animated version of *The Hobbit* by Gene Deitch. It was rushed through production and had little to do with the original story. The first animated movie of *The Lord of the Rings*, an adaptation of the first half, was produced by Saul Zaentz in 1978, with mixed reviews.

About twenty years later, Peter Jackson, a movie director from New Zealand, seemed to initially agree with Tolkien that *The Lord of the Rings* was impossible to film. The world described by Tolkien was just too vast to portray with images. Also, *The Lord of the Rings* is not a single story. Besides the saga of Frodo, there are many other stories going on, which could easily become confusing in a movie script. But when Jackson was able to acquire the movie rights from Zaentz, he took on the challenge.

Unlike other directors before him, Jackson was able to employ new digital technologies that allowed him to overcome some obstacles, such as portraying large battle scenes or showing creatures of different sizes standing next to each other. Jackson released *The Fellowship of the Ring* in 2001, *The Two Towers* in 2002, and *The Return of the King* in 2003. The last of these three won eleven Oscars. The success he received encouraged him to produce a series of movies adapting *The Hobbit* from 2012 to 2014.

Some of Tolkien's fans complained that Jackson's movie skipped some scenes, added others, changed some important details, and emphasized the battles much more than Tolkien had done in his books. They didn't think he stayed faithful to the spirit of Tolkien's books, even though he worked hard on the details, including much of the amazing scenery (thanks to the artwork of Ted Nasmith, John Howe, and Alan Lee).

Some people read the books before watching the movies, while others did the opposite. In any case, Jackson's movies caused an increase in book sales. And even those who have never read the books now know many of Tolkien's characters and famous quotes due to the movies' popularity.

TOLKIEN MANIA

Since the first edition of *The Hobbit,* the number of Tolkien's fans has continued to grow. Readers began to discuss his books in conferences and magazines and formed clubs and societies. The first known Tolkien club was formed in 1960 by a group of Los Angeles fans, who, for a short time,

published a fanzine called *I-Palantir.* The Tolkien Society of America sprung up soon after, followed by other chapters of the society around the world.

Moving beyond a simple discussion of Tolkien's books, some fans organized societies for the study of Elvish languages. The first of these societies was the Elvish Linguistic Fellowship (ELF), which has produced several publications.

Most recently, the Internet and social media have contributed to the multiplication of these societies all over the world, so that every Tolkien fan can connect with others to find information and join discussions. Even the academic world, which initially looked down on Tolkien's books as children's stories, has become more interested in his literary style and the connection between his books and his Medieval research.

(below left) **A participant at the Middle Earth Festival dressed as a Black Rider.**
Paul Lucas, Flickr

(below right) **A participant at the Middle Earth Festival dressed as an orc.**
Paul Lucas, Flickr

The explosion of Tolkien societies has also produced a great number of festivals in celebration of the author and his books. One of these is the Middle Earth Festival, where participants enjoy a weekend of food, songs, book readings, games, and activities for young and old (including reenactment of battles). This festival has been held every year until 2018, when it had to stop temporarily for lack of funds.

Besides societies and festivals, Tolkien fans have enjoyed a host of Middle-earth-inspired games. Some of these featured the quest of the hobbits, others focused on the battles, and others, such as the first version of War of the Ring, are a combination of both.

Even popular videogames and role-playing games such as Dungeons and Dragons have been influenced by *The Lord of the Rings*. The first licensed videogame based on Tolkien's work was *The Hobbit,* the first of *The Tolkien Trilogy* (published in America and Australia as *The Tolkien Software Adventure Series*).

Action figures have also filled the stores, and even Lego has come up with a series of building-block sets and figurines inspired by *The Hobbit* and *The Lord of the Rings*.

A LASTING LEGACY

One of Tolkien's most important legacies is opening the door to a seemingly infinite world that others can explore. And while many readers have simply enjoyed this exploration in the pages of Tolkien's books, others have explored further through writing, music, and art.

Even though Tolkien was certainly not the first to write fantastical tales and homemade myths, his success has helped establish fantasy as a distinct, recognized genre, and has made it easier for other authors of the same genre to get their books published. He has also left an example to emulate, with his well-organized "secondary world," his complex stories, and his fascinating characters. Many fantasy authors such as J. K. Rowling and George R. R. Martin and filmmakers such as George Lucas have admitted their debt to Tolkien.

Indeed, many artists have found in Tolkien's work the inspiration they need. Some said that painting Middle-earth is like discovering a true

Lego figures of Gandalf and Legolas. *Spielbrick Films, CC BY 2.0*

J·R·R·TOLKIEN · THE LORD OF THE RINGS

J. R. R. Tolkien (1892 - 1973)

"home," a place that everyone longs for but that has never before been described in such detail. "There's nothing quite like finding something important you didn't know you were looking for!" artist Ted Nasmith says on his website.

The same goes for music. Chris Seeman, one of the main authorities on Tolkien-inspired music, has counted thousands of compositions based on Tolkien's books, with the most popular songs and tunes being the ones that have accompanied dramatizations, such as the 1981 BBC radio series and Peter Jackson's movies in particular.

But Tolkien's inspiration is not limited to writers, artists, and musicians. By opening the doors to such a rich and detailed world as Middle-earth, Tolkien encouraged everyone to keep exploring and imagining the possibility of a nobler life that brings new meaning to daily tasks. And by making his world genuinely credible, he gave hope that such a life can be more than a dream.

While most fads come and go, the majority of Tolkien's fans remain faithful for life. Many reread his works from time to time, finding them appropriate for whatever situation they might be facing. That's because, by leading weak and simple hobbits through a "subcreation" filled with all the beauty and foulness, virtues and vices, emotions and convictions of this world, he helped his readers to identify with their journey. The hobbits—and the reader with them—learn lessons of friendship, courage, and self-sacrifice, both by experience and through the advice of wise friends like Gandalf, Samwise, and the Elves. Tolkien helped his readers to look at reality both objectively and hopefully, driven by the assurance that each person is part of a greater story, where good, ultimately, will triumph.

(left) **A 2004 UK postage stamp with a map of a portion of Middle-earth.** *Picture Lake, iStock*

(right) **A 2017 postage stamp printed in Kyrgystan, styled after a photo of J. R. R. Tolkien.** *Olga Popova, Shutterstock*

ACKNOWLEDGMENTS

Writing this book has put me in contact with a great number of enthusiastic Tolkien fans who have been glad to help me in many ways. I have always loved exploring Tolkien's worlds. I just never realized how many people, like me, refuse to believe the world we see with our eyes is all there is.

I thank all those who have thoughtfully taken the time to read my drafts, including my dear friend and fellow author Bradley Steffens and my equally dear friends, editors, and Tolkien fans Dan Saxton and Timothy Massaro. I am deeply indebted to John Garth, author of *Tolkien and the Great War* and *The Worlds of J. R. R. Tolkien*, for patiently answering my numerous questions and giving me recommendations, and to Wayne Hammond, coauthor of *The Lord of the Rings: A Reader's Companion*, who has taken the time to direct me during one of my inquiries. A special thanks goes to my son, Angelo Kevin, a teacher's aide in Portland, Oregon, who has helped me with ideas for the activities in this book.

GLOSSARY

allegory: a symbolic way of representing a true object, person, or idea

Anglican: related to the established Church of England

armistice: a temporary pause in fighting, due to an agreement of the parties at war

aviary: a large place (usually a cage) where birds are kept

battalion: a military unit

budgerigar: a type of parrot

calligraphy: decorative handwriting

casualty: a person who is hurt or killed or goes missing in war or during an accident or disaster

Celtic: related to the Celts, an ancient European population

chutney: a thick sauce, usually made of pickled, sweetened fruits with spices; originally from India, it became popular in England as a condiment, especially for meats

cul-de-sac: a street that is closed at one end

disown: to refuse to accept a natural relationship, usually after an offense (for example, an offended father can refuse to accept a girl as his daughter)

elf: in common language, an elf is a small creature, usually with pointed ears and magical powers, and traditionally considered mischievous; for Tolkien, the Elves were the first race of the Children of Ilúvatar (before Men and Dwarves), and were beautiful, noble, and immortal

Elven: related to Elves

Elvish: related to Elves; while some have made a distinction between *Elven* ("related to Elves") and *Elvish* ("related to the language of Elves"), Tolkien uses them interchangeably in most of his works

epic: a long poem, usually telling the story of a hero or heroine

etymology: the study of the origins of words

eucatastrophe: a word invented by Tolkien for the good, unexpected turn of events that bring a story to a happy ending

Faëry: for Tolkien, the magical world where mythical creatures live and where men and women sometimes intrude

fairy: in common language, a fairy is a small creature with magical powers; Tolkien only mentions them in early writings, sometimes as another name for Elves

foie gras: a luxury product made of fattened duck or goose liver

gnome: in common language, a dwarf that lives inside the earth; for Tolkien, the Gnomes were a race of Elves.

Gothic: the language once spoken by the Goths, an ancient East Germanic population

insulin: a hormone produced in the pancreas to regulate the amount of glucose in the blood; an animal-derived or synthetic form of insulin is used to treat diabetes

loft: upper room or attic

marmalade: a sweet jelly, usually made of bitter oranges, including the peels

Middle-earth: in Tolkien's books, it's a mythological place that existed in a time long past

Morse code: a code used internationally in order to transmit signals; characters are represented by a combination of dots and dashes, which can be expressed through electrical pulses (short for dots and long for dashes)

myth: a story that was told in an ancient culture to explain mysterious events, which usually involved beings with supernatural powers and fantastical events

ogre: in fairy tales, a terrifying and destructive giant

oratory: in the Roman Catholic Church, a place of prayer and the community of priests who live there

Orc: a warlike creature of Middle-earth fighting for the forces of evil; Tolkien used the words *orc* and *goblin* interchangeably

philologist: a person who studies how words are created, developed, and used

philology: the study of words (literally, "love for words")

porcelain: a hard, white, delicate substance made by baking clay

porridge: hot cereal

punt: a long, narrow, flat-bottomed boat, usually moved with a pole

ration: a fixed amount of food, often distributed during wartime or a disaster

reader: in British universities, a senior teacher, with a rank just below that of a professor

rector: the head of a university or school

regiment: a military unit that is usually made of several battalions

reserve: a military force that is kept from action until a later time

rheumatic fever an inflammatory disease that may occur when strep throat is not treated

royalties: a share of profits given to the owner of a property (including intellectual property, such as copyright)

sacrament: a Christian ceremony (such as baptism or the Lord's Supper) that is believed to convey grace and represent a spiritual reality

saga: a long story about past heroes, usually from Norway and Iceland

scholar: a person who has studied a subject for a long time and knows it well

scholarship: money given to a student to pay for his education

sedentary: not physically active

seminarian: a person who is training to become a priest, minister, or rabbi

signaling: using signals to send communications

soufflé: a baked egg dish

stalactite: a pointed piece of rock that hangs down from the roof of a cave

tram: a vehicle that runs on rails for transportation of people within a city

typhoid: a serious, contagious disease

valedictory: related to or expressing a goodbye; from the Latin, meaning "saying farewell"

Welsh: the language spoken in Wales

RESOURCES TO EXPLORE

BOOKS FOR FURTHER STUDY

BOOKS BY TOLKIEN

Tolkien, J. R. R. *Letters from Father Christmas*. Boston: Houghton Mifflin, 1999.

Tolkien, J. R. R. *Roverandom*, ed. Christina Scull and Wayne G. Hammond. Boston: Houghton Mifflin, 1999.

Tolkien, J. R. R. *Tales from the Perilous Realm*. Boston: Houghton Mifflin, 2008.

Tolkien, J. R. R. *The Annotated Hobbit*, ed. Douglas A. Anderson. Boston: Houghton Mifflin, 2002.

Tolkien, J. R. R. *The Hobbit*, audiobook, narrated by Rob Inglis. Boston: Houghton Mifflin, 2012.

Tolkien, J. R. R. *The Lord of the Rings: One Volume*. Boston: Houghton Mifflin, 2005.

Tolkien, J. R. R. *The Lord of the Rings Trilogy*, audiobook, narrated by Rob Inglis. Boston: Houghton Mifflin, 2002.

BOOKS ABOUT TOLKIEN

Carpenter, Humphrey. *J. R. R. Tolkien: A Biography*. London: Allen and Unwin, 1977. (NOTE: Not written for children, but any young reader who can enjoy *The Lord of the Rings* is ready for this full biography of Tolkien, which is the only one to be authorized by the Tolkien Trust.)

Collins, David R. *J. R. R. Tolkien*. Minneapolis: Lerner, 2005.

Gardner, Angela, ed. *Black and White Ogre Country: The Lost Tales of Hilary Tolkien*. Moreton-in-Marsh, UK: ADC Publications, 2009.

Garth, John. *The Worlds of J. R. R. Tolkien: The Places that Inspired Middle-Earth*. Princeton and Oxford: Princeton University Press, 2020. (NOTE: Not written for children, but the photographs are amazing and older children can read it slowly and gain a greater appreciation for Tolkien and his writings).

Hammond, Wayne G., and Christina Scull. *J. R. R. Tolkien: Artist and Illustrator*. London: HarperCollins, 1995. (NOTE: Not written for children, but interesting if you want to see his artwork.)

Hammond, Wayne G., and Christina Scull. *The Art of the Hobbit*. London: HarperCollins, 2012. (NOTE: Same as above.)

Hammond, Wayne G., and Christina Scull. *The Art of the Lord of the Rings*. London: HarperCollins, 2017. (NOTE: Same as above.)

Lynch, Doris. *J. R. R. Tolkien: Creator of Languages and Legends*. New York: Franklin Watts, 2003.

Tolkien, John and Priscilla. *The Tolkien Family Album*. London: HarperCollins, 1992.

Willett, Edward. *J. R. R. Tolkien: Master of Imaginary Worlds*. Berkeley Heights, NJ: Enslow Publishers, 2004.

ACTIVITY BOOKS

Oseland, Chris-Rachael. *An Unexpected Cookbook: The Unofficial Book of Hobbit Cookery*. CreateSpace Independent Publishing Platform, 2017.

MUSEUMS

Sarehole Mill

Birmingham Museums
Cole Bank Road
Birmingham, B13 0BD
London, England
The 250-year-old mill that Tolkien visited in Sarehole is now turned into a museum and bakery.

Marion E. Wade Center

Wheaton College
501 College Avenue
Wheaton, IL 60187
It includes a desk and some writing items that belonged to Tolkien.

WEBSITES

The Tolkien Society

Visit the links page (https://www.tolkiensociety.org/links/) for a long list of related websites.

HOLIDAYS AND ANNIVERSARIES

March 25: Annual Tolkien Reading Day, held by the Tolkien Society in honor of the destruction of the Ring and the fall of Sauron.

September 22: Birthday of Bilbo and Frodo. The week around this day is Tolkien Week—inaugurated in 1978 by the American Tolkien Society.

NOTES

CHAPTER 1: FROM AFRICAN DESERTS TO A LOST PARADISE

"How is Hell-in": Angela Gardner, ed., *Black and White Ogre Country: The Lost Tales of Hilary Tolkien* (Moreton-in-Marsh, UK: ADC Publications, 2009), 22.

CHAPTER 2: CHANGES AND HEARTBREAKS

"it was an effort": J. R. R. Tolkien, *Letters of J. R. R. Tolkien: A Selection,* ed. Humphrey Carpenter, with Christopher Tolkien (Boston: Houghton Mifflin, 1981), 264.

CHAPTER 3: UNDERGRADUATE

"joined all the Exeter societies": Philip Zaleski and Carol Zaleski, *The Fellowship: The Literary Lives of the Inklings* (New York: Farrar, Straus and Giroux, 2015), 58.

"porridge, eggs": John Garth, *Tolkien at Exeter College* (Oxford, UK: Exeter College, 2014), 9.

CHAPTER 4: WARTIME

"they had been granted": Tolkien, *Letters of J. R. R. Tolkien,* 10.

"like death": Bill Cater, "We Talked of Love, Death and Fairy Tales," *Daily Telegraph,* December 4, 2001, 23.

"far superior": Humphrey Carpenter, *J. R. R. Tolkien: A Biography* (Boston: Houghton Mifflin, 2000), 81.

CHAPTER 5: LOST TALES FOUND

"immeasurable sorrow": J. R. R. Tolkien, *The Silmarillion,* Second Edition, (Boston: Houghton Mifflin, 2001), 5.

"it seemed that": Tolkien, *The Silmarillion,* 5.

"make the theme": J. R. R. Tolkien, *The Book of Lost Tales*, vol. 1, (New York: Random House Publishing Group, 1983), 53.

CHAPTER 6: THERE LIVED A HOBBIT

"In a hole": J. R. R. Tolkien, *The Hobbit* (Boston: Houghton Mifflin Harcourt, 2012), 3.

"This book, with the help": Rick Gekoski, *Nabokov's Butterfly & Other Stories of Great Authors and Rare Books* (New York: Carroll & Graf Publishers, 2004), 22.

"of a very thin": Zaleski and Zaleski, *Literary Lives of the Inklings*, 240.

"like a coral insect": C. S. Lewis, *The Collected Letters of C. S. Lewis,* vol. 3, ed. Walter Hooper (New York: Harper Collins Publishers, 2007), 1579.

CHAPTER 7: THE LORD OF THE RINGS

"Keep up your hobbitry": Tolkien, *Letters of J. R. R. Tolkien*, 78.

"owe something": Tolkien, 303.

"as clear cut": Tolkien, 78.

"He drew a deep breath": J. R. R. Tolkien, *The Lord of the Rings: One Volume* (Boston: Houghton Mifflin Hartcourt, 2004), 1031.

"I am sure I did not invent him": Tolkien, *Letters of J. R. R. Tolkien*, 79.

"elvishly lovely": Humphrey Carpenter, *J. R. R. Tolkien: A Biography* (Boston: Houghton Mifflin, 2000), 222.

"super science fiction": Tolkien, *Letters of J. R. R. Tolkien*, 181.

"Joy beyond the walls": J. R. R. Tolkien, *The Tolkien Reader* (New York: Ballantine Books, 1966), 68.

"the conquest": C. S. Lewis, *On Stories and Other Essays on Literature* (Orlando, FL: Hartcourt Books, 1982), 83.

CHAPTER 8: RETIREMENT AND LEGACY

"a walking Christmas tree": Christina Scull and Wayne G. Hammond, *The J. R. R. Tolkien Companion & Guide* (London: Harper Collins Publishers, 2017), 489.

"I was terrified": Zaleski and Zaleski, *Literary Lives of the Inklings*, 503.

SELECTED BIBLIOGRAPHY

Carpenter, Humphrey. *J. R. R. Tolkien: A Biography*. London: Allen and Unwin, 1977.

Garth, John. *Tolkien and the Great War: The Threshold of Middle-Earth*. London: HarperCollins, 2002.

———. *Tolkien at Exeter College: How an Oxford Undergraduate Created Middle-earth*. Oxford: Exeter College, 2017.

———. *The Worlds of J. R. R. Tolkien: The Places That Inspired Middle-Earth*. London: Frances Lincoln, 2020.

Scull, Christina and Wayne G. Hammond. *The J. R. R. Tolkien Companion and Guide, 3 vols*. London, Harper Collins Publishers, 2017.

Shippey, T.A. *J. R. R. Tolkien: Author of the Century*. London: Allen and Unwin, 2000.

———. *The Road to Middle-Earth*. London: Allen and Unwin, 1982.

Tolkien, J. J. R. *Letters of J. R. R. Tolkien*, ed. Humphrey Carpenter, with Christopher Tolkien. London: Allen and Unwin, 1981.

Zaleski, Philip and Carol Zaleski. *The Fellowship: The Literary Lives of the Inklings*. New York: Farrar, Straus, and Giroux, 2015.

INDEX

Y

Z

ISBN 978-1-64160-138-2
$18.99 (CAN $24.99)

Code Cracking for Kids
Secret Communications Throughout History, with 21 Codes and Ciphers

By Jean Daigneau

"An engaging, hands-on approach to combine social studies and STEM." —Booklist Online

Throughout history, people have written coded messages to safeguard and pass along secret information and figured out ways to break the coded messages of their enemies and determine what they had planned. The study of these techniques is known as cryptology, and *Code Cracking for Kids* explores many aspects of this fascinating and exciting topic. Kids will read about famous people, such as Julius Caesar and Thomas Jefferson, who invented codes and ciphers; about military codes and codebreaking projects, including Allied efforts to crack Germany's infamous Enigma machine during World War II; and about work being done today by the US government and private-sector experts to safeguard our cybersecurity. Readers will also learn about unsolved ciphers throughout history, codes that can be found in our everyday lives, and devices used by governments and spies to conceal information.

Code Cracking for Kids includes a glossary, a list of online resources, and hands-on activities that allow kids to replicate early code devices and to learn several ciphers to encode and decode their own top-secret messages. Kids will:

* Encrypt a message using a dictionary cipher
* Create a cipher wheel like the one designed by Thomas Jefferson
* Make and write with invisible ink
* Hide a ciphered message inside an egg
* Learn the sounds of Morse code
* And more!

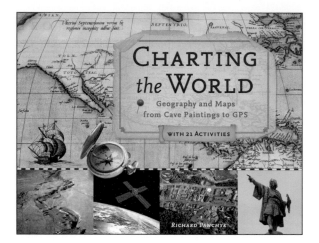

ISBN 978-1-56976-344-5
$18.95 (CAN $20.95)

Charting the World
Geography and Maps from Cave Paintings to GPS with 21 Activities
By Richard Panchyk

"The 21 side activities are enlightening and range widely in difficulty without requiring expensive or hard-to-get materials." —*Kirkus Reviews*

As soon as early humans began to scratch images on cave walls, they were creating maps. And while these first drawings were used to find hunting grounds or avoid danger, they later developed into far more complex navigational tools. *Charting the World* tells the fascinating history of maps and mapmaking, navigators and explorers, and the ways that technology has enhanced our ability to understand the world around us. Richly illustrated with full-color maps and diagrams, it gives children an in-depth appreciation of geographical concepts and principles and shows them how to unlock the wealth of information maps contain. It also features 21 hands-on activities for readers to put their new skills to the test.

Children will:

* Build a three-dimensional island model using a contour map
* Engrave a simple map on an aluminum "printing plate"
* Determine the elevation of hills in their neighborhood
* Draw a treasure map and have a friend search for the hidden stash
* Create a nautical chart of a small puddle
* Survey their backyard or local park
* Navigate a course using a compass
* And much more

Now more than ever, the study of geography is crucial to understanding our ever-changing planet, from political change and warfare to environmental conservation and population growth.

ISBN 978-1-61374-556-4
$18.99 (CAN $25.99)

World War I for Kids
A History with 21 Activities

By R. Kent Rasmussen

"Organized, thorough, and accessible. An engaging start for students learning about World War I." —*School Library Journal*

One hundred years after the "Great War," *World War I for Kids* provides an intriguing and comprehensive look at this defining conflict that involved all of the world's superpowers. Why and how did the war come about? What was daily life like for soldiers in the trenches? What roles did zeppelins, barbed wire, and the passenger ship *Lusitania* play in the war? Who were Kaiser Wilhelm, the Red Baron, and Edith Cavell? Young history buffs will learn the answers to these questions and many others, including why the western front bogged down into a long stalemate; how the war ushered in an era of rapid military, technological, and societal advances; and how the United States' entry helped end the war. Far from a dry catalog of names, dates, and battles, this richly illustrated book goes in depth into such fascinating topics as turn-of-the-20th-century weaponry and the important roles animals played in the war and explains connections among events and how the war changed the course of history. Hands-on activities illuminate both the war and the times.

Kids can:

* Make a periscope
* Teach a dog to carry messages
* Make a parachute
* Learn a popular World War I song
* Cook Maconochie stew, a common trench meal
* And much more

ISBN 978-1-56976-349-0
$16.95 (CAN $18.95)

Elizabeth I, the People's Queen
Her Life and Times, 21 Activities

By Kerrie Logan Hollihan

"This attractive entry in the For Kids series offers 21 activities to supplement the text and provide a sense of what Elizabethan England was all about." —*Kirkus Reviews*

Queen Elizabeth I learned to trust no one. Even before Elizabeth was crowned queen at the age of 25, her mother, Anne Boleyn, had been executed for treason by her father, King Henry VIII. She was then removed from the royal line of succession and later imprisoned in the Tower of London, accused of plotting to overthrow her sister, Queen Mary. Yet despite all the challenges to her power, she became a hero of the Church of England in a century when Catholics and Protestants burned one another at the stake, she spoke five languages in a day when few women were taught to read, and she led a nation where men proclaimed that women had no right to take part in public life. During Elizabeth's 45-year reign, English literature, theater, music, and culture flourished. And, after her navy defeated the Spanish armada, England's military power transformed the once tiny kingdom into a chief player among Europe's nations.

This lively biography of one of England's greatest monarchs includes a time line, online resources, and 21 activities to offer readers hands-on experiences with life in the Elizabethan Era. Kids can:

* Create costumes for the queen's court, including a knight's helmet, a neck ruff, and a cloak
* Play and sing a madrigal
* Create a 3-D map of an Elizabethan town
* Stitch a blackwork flower
* Design a family coat of arms
* Play a game of Nine Men's Morris
* Grow a knot garden
* And much more

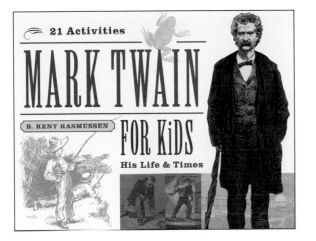

ISBN 978-1-55652-527-8
$14.95 (CAN $22.95)

Mark Twain for Kids
His Life & Times, 21 Activities

By R. Kent Rasmussen

"Appealing . . . a useful resource for teachers and student researchers." —*Children's Literature*

Nineteenth-century America and the world of Samuel L. Clemens, better known as Mark Twain, come to life as children journey back in time with this history- and literature-laden activity book. The comprehensive biographical information explores Mark Twain as a multi-talented man of his times, from his childhood in the rough-and-tumble West of Missouri to his many careers—steamboat pilot, printer, miner, inventor, world traveler, businessman, lecturer, newspaper reporter, and most important, author—and how these experiences influenced his writing. Twain-inspired activities include:

* Making printer's type
* Building a model paddlewheel boat
* Unmasking a hoax
* Inventing new words
* Cooking cornpone
* Planning a newspaper
* Observing people
* Writing maxims

An extensive resource section offers information on Twain's classics, such as *Tom Sawyer* and *The Adventures of Huckleberry Finn*, as well as a listing of recommended web sites to explore.

ISBN 978-1-55652-778-4

$18.99 (CAN $25.99)

Isaac Newton and Physics for Kids
His Life and Ideas with 21 Activities

By Kerrie Logan Hollihan

"Hollihan introduces readers to the scientific brilliance, as well as the social isolation, of this giant figure, blending a readable narrative with an attractive format that incorporates maps, diagrams, historical photographs, and physics activities." —*Booklist*

In a few short years, Isaac Newton made astounding discoveries in physics, astronomy, optics, and mathematics—yet never told a soul. Though isolated, snobbish, and jealous, he almost single-handedly changed the course of scientific advancement and ushered in the Enlightenment. Newton invented the refracting telescope, explained the motion of planets and comets, discovered the multicolored nature of light, and created calculus, a new field of mathematics. The world might have been a very different place had Netwon's theories and observations not been coaxed out of him by his colleagues.

Isaac Newton and Physics for Kids paints a rich portrait of this brilliant and complex man, including a time line, online resources, and 21 hands-on projects that explore the scientific concepts Newton developed and the times in which he lived.

Kids can:

 * Experiment with swinging pendulums
 * Create a 17th-century Plague mask
 * Track the phases of the moon
 * Bake an "apple pye in a coffin"
 * Test Newton's Three Laws of Motion using coins, a skateboard, and a model boat
 * Build a simple waterwheel
 * And much more

ISBN 978-1-61373-146-8
$16.95 (CAN $19.95)

Henry David Thoreau for Kids
His Life and Ideas with 21 Activities

By Corinne Hosfeld Smith

"Well organized and with plenty of grist for both minds and hands." —*Kirkus Reviews*

Henry David Thoreau is best known for living two years along the shores of Walden Pond in Concord, Massachusetts, and writing about his experiences in *Walden; or, Life in the Woods.* Today, more than 150 years later, people are still inspired by his thoughtful words and observations about individual rights, social justice, civil disobedience, and the natural world.

    Henry David Thoreau for Kids chronicles the short but influential life of this remarkable American thinker. In addition to learning about Thoreau's contributions to our culture, readers will participate in 21 engaging, hands-on projects that bring his ideas to life. Kids will:

* Build a model of the Walden cabin
* Keep a daily journal
* Plant a garden
* Bake trail-bread cakes
* Start a rock collection
* And much more!

    The book also includes a time line and list of resources—books, websites, and places to visit or explore online—that offer even more opportunities to connect with this fascinating author and naturalist.

CHICAGO REVIEW PRESS

Available at your favorite bookstore, by calling (800) 888-4741, or at www.chicagoreviewpress.com